JESUS WENT

QUESTIONS, IMPRESSIONS, AND CONSEQUENCES
OF GOING WHERE JESUS GOES

TIM HOLCOMB

BAREFOOT
NOMAD
Williamsburg, VA 23188

Barefoot Nomad Publishing
PO Box 5306 Williamsburg, VA 23188
BarefootNomadLLC@gmail.com

© 2018 by Tim Holcomb

Cover: Daniel Berry, 99designs.com

ISBN 978-1-7322204-0-9

For my dad,
who gave me the freedom to ask "Why not?"

For my mom,
who listens to my meandering ramblings.

For my kids,
who learned early to buckle up and hold on.

And for my bride,
who holds me with open hands
despite the chaos it brings into our lives.

Contents

What you should know first

The Age of Enlightenment in the 18th century elevated thought and reason to new heights with incredible global impact. It applied rational thinking and scientific approaches to all manner of issues: social, political, economic, philosophical, religious. It championed logic-based arguments, cause-and-effect relationships, and A+B=C clarity. The world changed.

Sometimes, though, that linear thinking which we have embraced can actually limit our understanding, for understanding comes not just from knowing the facts; it also comes from knowing the intangible but real soul of something. One important result of the Enlightenment was to open the doors of the Bible's meaning to us through great thinkers. However "what does it mean" and "what is it saying" are two equally important but different questions. One gives us knowledge, the other moves us. One teaches us about the text, the other invites us to let the text lead us somewhere.

In *Jesus Went*, it is my desire to allow texts and truths we have become familiar with do the latter – invite us. The style of writing I use is fluid and may seem disjointed, though if you look at it from a 30,000-foot view you'll see that invitation woven throughout. I am an analogy and metaphor guy. Very rarely will you get into a conversation with me that I don't use some word picture to describe a point I'm trying to make. That's how I've written this book. I hope we can look at the soul of the familiar. If you are looking for concrete action points or outlined lists, please return the book to the store, or at least don't write a review saying "OK, so what now?" That question I am unashamedly leaving between you and God. There are plenty of great books and programs that provide specifics of how individuals have answered that question for themselves and I eagerly endorse them. Some you'll find me referencing.

This book is like a bunch of kids looking at a high-dive board at a pool. They have a common goal – get over their fear and climb what seems like a million feet up onto a skinny platform. But once they each get to the top of the ladder, no two will jump off the high-dive the same way – some will flail arms, some will try to be as straight as a pencil while holding their nose, some will scream, and at least one kid will smack belly first. Each jumps in the water differently, but each had to get up the same ladder. That's what I'm hoping we do here, get up the ladder together. You're free to jump off how best suits you. The bigger issue isn't how you get into the water, but that you find it in you to climb the ladder, walk to the edge of the board, and launch out.

If you want a simple outline for this book and each chapter, it is this – questions should lead to impressions which should lead to consequences. What those impressions are and what consequences they lead each of us to next, I am hopeful in. Enjoy reading.

The gap between knowing and going

"All of us in the Coca-Cola family wake up each morning knowing that every single one of the world's 5.6 billion people will get thirsty that day…and that we are the ones with the best opportunity to refresh them….If we make it impossible for these 5.6 billion people to escape Coca-Cola…then we assure our future success for many years to come. Doing anything else is not an option."

Robert C. Goizueta
Chairman Board of Directors, CEO Coca-Cola
1993 Annual Report to stockholders[1]

And they are succeeding. In the past ten years I've visited twenty-seven countries and *everywhere* there have been two things I can always find. Coke and cell phones. I was driving in the sub-Sahara for several hours and stopped at a shack of four branches and palm leaves. Warm Coke. Himalayas? Coke. Back forests of Brazil? A whole Coke factory. Coke is doing it. In the next twenty-four hours, if anybody in the world gets thirsty, Coke can satisfy their thirst.

Jesus said something very similar sounding, albeit with a much different purpose and meaning than Coke. "If anyone is thirsty, let him come to me and drink."[2]

Why two thousand years later is it easier for a person to find Coke in my town, my country, or the world than it is to find Jesus?

~~~

I have a lot of books in my office. One day I decided to remove the ones that were predominately focused on theological explanations of the Great Commission (Matthew 28:18-20), reaching our world, the gospel, and *missio Dei* – the mission of God. All of these works are by great authors who have laid a foundation and continue to build my understanding of what the Bible says about the redemptive passion of God.

Then I took down the books that were loaded with stories about men and women who have done great things for God and the expansion of his Kingdom – biographies, books on living mission-focused wherever we are, accounts of secret believers in spiritually resistant countries. It didn't matter if they were on another continent or seeing people connect to God right in their own backyard, all of these inspire me. To be honest, they intimidate me too. These people's stories are most often ones I can't relate to, but wish I could.

So I sat on the floor between these two piles and thought *something* has to fit in between the "knowing" theological content and the "going" action content. Knowing something is true doesn't always motivate me to do it. I find myself sometimes stuck in that middle space: I know the spiritual reasons and responsibility I have to see that those not yet knowing Christ have a chance to hear about him, but I also pull back from many opportunities with my neighbors, family, people on my kids' sports teams, and in classes.

Much has been written about how the message of the gospel and the influence of biblical teaching have become marginalized and pushed to the edge of relevance in society, most noticeably in the U.S. and Europe. We who claim Christianity as our faith need to become more intentional in our actions about what being a follower of Jesus Christ means in our everyday interactions with those who don't follow Jesus if we do indeed want them to "come and drink". The biggest challenge today might be for the church to resist the pull to cocoon and isolate.

It was no different for the first believers. They were, after all, an odd sect within a minority religion that was dwarfed by an empire-wide pagan religion crafted from Greek gods and cultic beliefs. Minority groups in any context tend to look inward for survival within societies that don't accept them or their beliefs – it's human nature to desire that safety and acceptance. And yet these early believing communities thrived and grew in influence and number. How? What was said or seen that stuck with them to continue the work that Jesus laid out for them to do in an uninviting atmosphere? Malcolm Gladwell wrote in his book *The Tipping Point*, "The specific quality that a message needs to be successful is the quality of 'stickiness.' Is the message – or the food, or the movie, or the product – memorable? Is it so memorable, in fact, that it can create change, that it can spur someone to action?"[3] So, what was impressed on people who heard and experienced things firsthand with Jesus? What compelled them to go against the cultural norm of their day? How did they continue seeing God's Kingdom expand into the communities around them? To use Gladwell's words, what stuck that made a difference in what they did?

~~~

In the church, often we read our Bibles asking "Where's the command I'm supposed to obey?" or look in other books for steps to take and formulas to follow. But when we become so focused on the formula, we ignore letting God nudge us towards what he wants *us* specifically to do. We've become satisfied being spoon-fed concrete next steps, but those very things we find listed out many times don't really affect our core so they don't stick long term.

Let me give you a visual, one that once you see it you'll say, "Well, obviously."

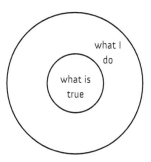

In the center circle is what I really believe, sometimes called our worldview. It's what is really real to me, my core convictions. The outer circle is what I do as a result of what I believe is true, the visible evidence and actions that come from who I am at the core.

When I read a book, listen to a talk or watch a movie, the author/speaker/director is trying to get his message into the core of who I am so that it then affects what I do. He may have some specific action in mind he could suggest, but if he *really* wants to see his intended message go viral, he needs to avoid having me look to *his* specific action points as the sole takeaway and miss the unique way that *I* am supposed to see that belief become action. He doesn't know my situation, my friends, my town or my shortcomings or skills. Those affect what I *do* once I know what I *believe*.

How a message gets to the core is done in several ways. For Christians, we look primarily to the Bible, and the Bible communicates to us in many ways. Narratives. Poetry. Lists of instructions and commands. Jesus himself used multiple methods, sometimes giving direct points, but more often than we realize he used stories. An amazing 90% of what we have recorded of Jesus' words is in story form – a parable, analogy, metaphor, word picture. I believe the reason was because stories and images leave impressions on us. They have stickiness and get to our core. And when they stick, we start seeing them shape our thinking, and then they begin to shape our actions.

This book is not one that mines the deep, rich theology that surround Jesus' words. As I said, there are plenty of authors who do that much better than I am capable of. This is my attempt to share several different theological truths about God's heart for his world that have moved from intellectual agreements to vivid images for me – impressions that God uses to fill that middle space and make theology personal, graspable, and memorable. We are a people who like images to hold onto – to remind us of truths and to provide clarity to things that seem abstract. They make it easier for us to understand things, so questions like "Do I really want to go where Jesus is going?" become internal and we can answer from our gut. That is when our theology becomes actionable. Said another way, impressions produce consequences.

My use of the word *impression* is intentional, specifically how it is used to describe someone working with something like wood or leather. When a craftsman puts a decorative mark onto a wooden chair, that indentation becomes a permanent part of the chair. The wood can't go back to its original condition and the chair's look is forever different. A man working in leather will leave his seal on the saddle or jacket or ladies handbag. It becomes a permanent identifying mark of the craftsman and his work. These two things – a permanent change, and the craftsman's identity – are what I believe God wants us to experience when we read Scripture rather than to simply have an opinion about it.

~~~

I believe there's a difference between a journey and a quest. A journey has a clear finishing point. You prepare for it, plan on how to best get there, and set your sites on it as you head out. A quest is something entirely different. You know what you are looking for, but aren't sure where you'll end up or what will happen along the way, and often you are different as a result of the quest. A journey takes you on a well-marked path around the woods. A quest takes you deep into the woods and the swamps and the cliffs and the caves and the fast-flowing rivers. A journey is known, seeking to avoid uncertainty. A quest is uncharted, created by curiosity. Isn't *quest*ion-asking as much about the process of finding an answer as much as getting the answer itself? The things learned along the process can expand our knowledge or ability more than the actual answer! Albert Einstein said, "Logic will get you from A to Z. Imagination will get you everywhere." This book is written to use the biblical text to prompt some questions that don't have narrow answers. How we answer those will be unique to each of us, coming from what is impressed upon you. From there, I do believe impressions have consequences which each of us will see in our individual God-led actions.

There is no pretense of this being a completed process for me, but I share some of the thoughts and images I've encountered along this quest that have become both dangerous and inviting at the same time, and have had a nasty tendency of not leaving me alone. They continue to influence my understanding of evangelism and missions, the church, decisions my wife and I make, my career, my time, what I pray for, what I talk to my kids about, where I give money, and countless other things. Jesus continues shaping me today, just as much as he did two thousand years ago with others.

~~~

Think of a car commercial. Any car commercial. For three seconds. Most likely you don't need that much time. Let me guess. You had an image of a silver or black car driving about thirty miles per hour over the speed limit on a windy road overlooking a cliff with the ocean below on a sunny day and nobody else on the road. It's probably a car that costs more than you can afford. The commercial ends with a camera sweep across the front of the car as it is parked at an angle on a black stage with two bright backdrop spotlights.

Great. Now can you name the make and model?

I'm sitting here watching Monday Night Football and every third commercial has been for a car. But I swear I couldn't give you the make and model of a single one. So was the commercial a success? Nope. A commercial is worth the money spent to make it only if it moves the viewer to respond. There has to be a call to action that triggers emotions, raises desires, or resonates with held values. If it lulls me to sleep, is entirely predictable, or I can't remember the specific product, it isn't successful. And even if it's memorable, if people aren't moved to buy the car, the beer, the low fat yogurt, or go to the restaurant, it isn't successful.

Too often I read the Bible like I watch commercials. I'm kind of bored, so I don't listen to what it's saying. I know what's coming, so I kind of tune out and use half my brain to sort through my to-do list for today. It's predictable and doesn't move me.

Sometimes there is a curse in knowing what we know. I know what Jesus said. I know the Great Commission. I know why Jesus came and I know that I'm supposed to help others in my neighborhood and in other places know that as well. We know it, agree with it, and have the talking points.

But if there's no response to a call to action, then the message didn't have an impact. The Great Commission becomes another commercial. The biblical encounters of Jesus with people become merely events that occur in a bigger story of which we are already familiar. So I miss so much that's right in front of my eyes, both in the Bible and its connection to what is being lived out right in front of me today.

What we're talking about is really the difference between opinions, beliefs, and convictions. Each of us has millions of opinions, thousands of beliefs, but probably only a few convictions. The difference between a belief and a conviction is that a conviction is a belief we hold so strongly that it consistently affects our actions. It consistently dictates what I will do. I have many opinions about things in the Bible, and a good number of beliefs grounded in biblical truths, but honestly only a handful of genuine convictions. The process of an opinion becoming a belief and then becoming conviction is an individual journey by necessity; otherwise it would not have stickiness in our life.

It was mid-February. I was a senior and it was the unavoidable time when I had to decide what was going to happen when I graduated. There were three options I was looking at: interviewing for jobs that would use my civil engineering degree, pursuing Officer Candidate School with one of the military branches, or go into full-time ministry. I had the paperwork for all three on the desk in my dorm room. And to be honest, I was tired of thinking through the pros and cons of each. None of them were *bad* decisions. Actually, the problem was that whichever of the three directions I considered, there were clear positives.

So I went for a midnight walk, ending up on top of the chapel on campus, sitting on the wall, my rear getting numb, staring across a large field in the middle of campus at nothing in particular. It started to snow. I just wanted to know something from God, but all I got was cold and silence.

I started reading Matthew, which was just as good as anything else to read that night. When I was done with chapter nine, I tried to move onto ten, but couldn't. Something I had read kept nagging me. I felt like I had to go back and read the last few sentences of chapter nine again, and again, and again.

Matthew had been with Jesus for three years. He had watched him, listened to him, sat around fires with him, asked him questions, slept under trees and walked down roads with him. He had seen him heal people, teach people, pray, rebuke, and clarify. He had seen people follow him, leave him, criticize him, cry out for him, and be changed by him. That much proximity and intimacy had an impact on Matthew. It began developing convictions within him.

If you read something long enough, you eventually see things you've missed the other hundred and fifty times you've read it. There were four questions that began to take shape as I read and reread a Jewish tax collector's recollections on spending so many days with Jesus…

Will I do as
Jesus did?

Jesus went through all the towns and
villages, teaching in their synagogues,
proclaiming the good news of the
kingdom and healing every disease and
sickness.

Do I see as
Jesus saw?

When he saw the crowds, he had
compassion on them, because they
were harassed and helpless, like sheep
without a shepherd.

Do I feel as
Jesus felt?

Then he said to his disciples, "The
harvest is plentiful but the workers are
few. Ask the Lord of the harvest,
therefore, to send out workers into his
harvest field."

Will I pray as
Jesus prayed?

Matthew 9:35-38, NIV

Do I see as Jesus saw?
Do I feel as Jesus felt?
Will I pray as Jesus prayed?
Will I do as Jesus did?

Over time, these simple questions from reading the first-hand account of one of Jesus' closest followers began to make the backstory of Jesus' life and the challenges he gave to us much more real, not slogans or catchy phrases. I believe the answers are supposed to leave an impression upon the church today. They provide the ingredients that can grow into a conviction and are the substance of an invitation.

All quests begin with questions. What's over there? What's around that bend? What will I discover? Nobody makes you ask these questions. They come from something that you chose to look at and linger until you have to find answers. Not answers for anybody else, but for yourself, your answers. Every important decision made is preceded by disturbing questions like these, ones which can't be easily shaken. They create a dissonance we choose not to ignore. They invite us to go on.

Do I see as Jesus saw?

Jesus went through the towns and villages. That statement alone says a lot. Jesus could have set up a rabbinical school to teach the religiously curious who would come seeking his insight and wisdom, but he didn't. He could have gone into the wilderness and lived the life of an odd religious recluse and proclaim his teaching to whoever would show up, but he didn't. He could have set up a healing center, a prophecy telling booth, or a carpenter's shop, but he didn't do any of these.

Jesus went to towns and villages. Not for adventure seeking or to satisfy wanderlust cravings – he sought after people. He visited great flourishing cities and poor obscure villages. And wherever he went, his presence was attractive. All sorts of people – rich, poor, citizens, slaves, soldiers, zealots, sinners – with all sorts of reasons came to hear him speak. He was around people.

Jesus was *constantly* inviting people to believe something bigger than they allowed themselves permission to, and his invitation came through explaining that the good kingdom of God was coming, and soon. This was in stark contrast to the people's lives marked by searching and longing and suffering until the thing they were searching for was found. C.S. Lewis wrote that our desire for something better – this disturbing restlessness – is a gift. This desire reminds us that we aren't complete or satisfied, and that there is something we hope to gain. "Creatures are not born with desires unless satisfaction for those desires exists," Lewis says. "A baby feels hunger; well, there is such a thing as food. A duckling wants to swim; well, there is such a thing as water. Men feel sexual desire; well, there is such a thing as sex. If I find in myself a desire which no experience in this world can satisfy, the most probable explanation is that I was made for another world."[4]

Whatever Jesus was telling people about centuries ago *was* attractive. Otherwise there wouldn't have been crowds following him. People wanted to find something. Good news is seen as good news when it is not considered the norm, or when it stands in stark contrast to something that isn't valued as good. It's "good" because it's in the midst of something "bad". In the third chapter of Genesis, the first book in the Bible, God's creation – animals, oceans, humans, plants, mosquitoes – exist as God intended and designed them. But then something happened that disrupted it all. God had given the first man and woman many things to do and only one not to do; but they couldn't avoid not doing that one thing. Consequences followed. The relationships that God designed were broken. Humanity's relationship with God was compromised. Relationships with other people took on shadows of fear where people tried to hide their guilt. The intimacy of marriage was now invaded by shame and blame. Social injustices took place within a few short years as the population grew and people dominated others in all manner of ways. The responsibility of stewardship that God gave man over the earth was challenged. Things were broken. Nothing was right.

The whole Old Testament is about God preparing for restoration of all these relationships. People for centuries waited in anticipation. They were eager for it. THIS is what Jesus came to talk about – the restoration of the ultimate relationship – between people and God – that had been missing since creation. God in Christ came to reclaim and put back in right order all that belongs to God and is currently broken, beginning with the God-Man relationship then rippling to the rest of a broken creation. This was the Good News Jesus talked about in houses, on the road, on hillsides, and in boats pushed offshore, and in every town and village.

We ache for a better world.[5]

We will be unsatisfied until our searching is done, and we will keep searching until we either find "it" or we accept that there is no "it" out there that will satisfy us. When my daughter is doing math homework and can't get the answer and is surrounded by balled up scrap paper with scribbled out attempts, she pushes her book across the table, and puts her head on her arms on the table. "I'll never get this…" and then the downward spiral starts. "I can't figure this out. I'm not smart enough. I'll never get this. It's impossible." She feels like a failure. As trivial as math homework sounds compared to the longings of the soul, the point is clear. Something she longs for deeply seems so elusive.

~~~

In the West, we let words be defined rather than alive. When we hear a word, it has a boundary of meaning to help us understand the concept and we accept the status quo definition without really thinking about it. But we know words imply much more than what can be possibly defined. As a simple example, I love my wife, but it's much more than can be described by a dictionary definition of "feelings of affection and attraction." Feelings of affection and attraction have not kept us married for twenty-five years. Like *love*, all words pulsate with meaning that comes from the speaker, the surroundings, and the context or bigger picture. Matthew used words in this way.

When Jesus was with people, he saw them in very specific conditions of aching and longing and searching and failing. It isn't any stretch of the imagination to think that three years of being in villages, seeing people, and talking with Jesus gave Matthew and the other eleven disciples intense insight into how Jesus really saw people. And the two words that Matthew chose to use describing how Jesus saw them are *harassed* and *helpless*. Two extreme words. Words that could have been used like hurting or wanting or empty somehow fell short.

Harassed is one of those words we use, but don't think about the meaning. It's a weighty word that has a sense of ongoing torment, an incessant chipping away that erodes the safety a person feels. Victims of harassment don't only worry about being physically or emotionally hurt; they have to deal with the unrelenting fear of the inevitable next encounter.

Most of us have never faced the continual wearing down of harassment. The closest I've ever come was condensed into a few minutes one night in Washington, D.C. after my dad's funeral.

My dad is buried in Arlington National Cemetery. He received full military honors at his funeral. Some images from that day stay with me. A caisson pulling his casket to his burial site. The sailors saluting his flag-draped casket. A squad of sailors firing three rounds of seven shots. The flag presented to my mom. Each grandkid putting a rose on grandpa's casket. Except my three year old son. He pulled out a rock and put it on top. He and grandpa liked throwing rocks in the river.

A bugler played Taps. I walked over to where the guns had fired and gathered as many of the spent casings as I could find. We walked back to the cars. My oldest son held my hand. The rest of the events of the day I don't really remember. I was emotionally done.

That night I couldn't sleep. We had all six of us in one hotel room and I remember slowly watching the clock digits change while everybody else slept. After 1AM, I couldn't take lying there anymore. I quietly left the room, rode the elevator down, and walked onto the street. Near our hotel was the Marine Iwo Jima Memorial. I just wanted a place I could wander in circles, letting thoughts and tears flow, so I headed there.

I was in my own world and didn't notice the two men until they were about a hundred feet away and coming from opposite directions. Nobody else was around. I turned to another sidewalk but I heard them change direction and follow.

I started back to the road and I heard their footsteps not too far behind me. Sound carries at night so I wasn't exactly sure how far back they were. When I took the next corner, my pace picked up a bit. A few seconds later I heard them walking around the corner.

I went a couple blocks more then looked back down the street before rounding the corner. They were one block away standing there looking at me. My pulse sped up incredibly.

When I got to the end of the block, I looked back and saw one man coming down the street…alone. *Where's the other?!* My mind started thinking of what I could do if somebody suddenly stepped in front of me. My heart was pounding. My thumb dialed 911 and stayed on the call button. My eyes were darting around.

Another intersection and I started sprinting. I knew the hotel was right around here but I was turned around and scared. *Leave me alone! I just buried my Dad!* Some running footsteps were behind me and when I turned, I saw two shapes still looking in my direction. I didn't look back anymore. Sprinting the next couple blocks, I found the hotel, and collapsed on the front steps, wheezing, sweaty, crying, and whispering "Please…just leave me alone…" to the phantom feeling that someone still hovered, watching from the shadows.

I can't imagine living in constant fear like that. But that's the word Matthew uses to describe how he understands Jesus seeing people. Harassed. Am I really willing to see people as Jesus sees them? Beyond the surface. Beyond the obvious. To look past the safeguards they put up? Will I stop to think of what is harassing them? The fear they have? The shame that shadows them? The guilt, the loneliness, the whispers? The desire to say from their deepest gut "Please…just leave me alone…" to whatever is stalking them?

Constant pressure against our thin walls of hope wears us down. We attempt to stand up and we think of how we will dig deep to find heroic superhuman willpower, but we start caving in again. We don't just *feel* helpless. We *are* helpless. This is the other word Matthew uses to describe what Jesus saw deep inside people around him.

We think of *helpless* in terms of semi-cute dependency, like a baby or a kitten or a just hatched bird in a nest.

That's not the way Matthew uses the word. This word is not a casual word. It is raw, emotional, emphatic desperation.

Old maritime literature describes different types of punishments given to sailors at sea. For some offenses the captain might decide to toss a man overboard. Imagine this man. The captain gives the order and several strong arms grab the doomed sailor. He's picked up, dragged across the wooden deck, and thrown over the rails.

A few seconds later he comes up for air, yelling, instinctively swimming back towards the ship. But the ship has rigged its sails and is moving. The man swims faster, madly hoping to catch up, that somebody will toss a line to him, but quickly he realizes that's a dying man's hope.

He stops, treading water, and screams. "PLEASE! HELP ME!" He can see the other sailors on the boat watching him but doing nothing more.

The waves make the man bob up and down in the water. His arms and legs continue kicking and flailing to keep his head above water. When he's on top of a wave, he can still see the boat, but then a wave lowers him. His head goes under and he gasps for air when he comes back up. The next wave carries him to its crest. He can still see the boat, but it's further away.

His arms are getting tired. They're burning now. It's getting harder to breath. He gulps some salt water, which makes him gag and thrash. A wave picks him up. The only thing he can see is the boat, slowly getting further and further and further away, until there's nothing left but him and the rising and falling waves. There's no hope for him.

The ancient word used to describe what this sailor is experiencing as he is thrown overboard and then watches the ship sail away is *rhiptó*. It translates to "helpless", the same word Matthew chooses to use.

You get a sense of the emotional weight of the word when Luke uses it in the book of Acts to describe a ship full of seasoned sailors and Roman soldiers tossing cargo overboard after two days of being battered by a huge storm in hopes of saving their ship. Then, on the third day, they've gotten to the point of desperation and throw the ship's tackle and other essential equipment overboard to lighten it more, hoping to survive. I doubt it was a simple casual flip overboard, but instead loud grunts tossing it as far out as possible, as if saying "Get this stuff away from here or we'll die!" even as in their guts they sense there is no hope of making it. The action and emotion behind tossing these things overboard is *rhiptó*. They are helpless even as they do it.[6]

It is also the same word that Jesus uses in Luke 17. "Things that cause people to sin are bound to come, but woe to that person through whom they come. It would be better for him to be *thrown into the sea* with a millstone tied around his neck than for him to cause one of these little ones to sin."[7] That person is *rhiptó*, helpless.

The same word Matthew used to explain how Jesus saw people as he walked with them.

~~~

Are these extreme words – harassed and helpless – really the right ones Matthew should have used? Our reserved receptivity to their use is maybe soothed a bit when we read the next description of people. Sheep. There is nothing disturbing about sheep. They are placid, docile, calm, and cute. Sheep are used to decorate babies' rooms. We like this softer image.

But sheep are completely helpless. I've asked shepherds on three continents about their sheep and have been told the same stories, so there must be something in the genetic code of sheep that makes them universally destitute. More than one shepherd told me that he had sheep who stood in a dirt patch woefully bleating because there was no more grass immediately around them, even though grass was only fifty feet away, until the shepherd came and prodded them. A shepherd in Asia told me some of his sheep had drowned during rainstorms because they had looked up to the sky and water had filled their nostrils. I've never heard of a sheep taking down a wolf, yet I've heard of sheep standing by watching a wolf take down another sheep. People in Jesus' day understood sheep. Sheep are stupid and helpless and defenseless. But, when they hear the voice of the shepherd, they respond. They come towards the sound of safety.

So as Jesus went through out towns and villages, he challenged his followers. "Do you see as I see?" Am I willing to go past appearances and see the helplessness, the hurt and the harassment that so many people are experiencing around me?

Do I feel as Jesus felt?

One in four pregnancies ends in a miscarriage. Our first one happened on a cross-country trip.

We had found out a few weeks earlier that Kath was pregnant with our first child and we were doing all the things you're supposed to do, like reading *What to Expect When You're Expecting*, eating mountains of broccoli, and nicknaming the baby Hampton since we found out Kath was pregnant while we were in Hampton Beach, New Hampshire.

Early in July, we loaded up our Toyota and headed west towards Colorado for work. We kept babbling like first-time parents do. We made it to Kath's folks in Ohio. Then the bleeding started.

The doctor ordered an ultrasound and we saw Hampton on the screen. There was our eleven week in utero child with a huge head, the family chin, and a long umbilical cord plugging him in like an extension cord to a Christmas tree. The arms and legs looked like little nubs. One nub was constantly moving back and forth towards the head, like Hampton was tossing popcorn into his mouth.

Then the doctor gave us the medical diagnosis. "There's a problem…" The image on the screen seemed to go from color and life to gray instantly. It doesn't matter if you're pro-life or pro-choice, there's nothing that prepares you for the emotions that come when a doctor says, "I'm sorry. There's nothing I can do. We need to do a D&C…"

I had never heard of a D&C, but I heard "surgery" and "remove" to know clearly what was going to happen. I don't remember what he said after that.

I remember Kath being in tears. The doctor rambled on sounding distant in my head. Some barely audible noise in a tunnel that I wasn't supposed to be in. I had a flurry of thoughts, and none of them brought comfort. Just more confusion, questions, emptiness.

The ultrasound of Hampton was still on the screen. He was right there! We had pictures of him! My mind was exploding and I screamed in my head "THAT'S MY CHILD!" And there was nothing I could do to help him. I cried.

God created us. He created us to be in relationship with him. He didn't create us to perform for him, or because he was bored and needed something to do, or because he was an extravert needing someone to talk to. He created us to be with him. He knows we're screwed up, but he loves us anyways. He knows all our potential and he watches us daily. We are made in his image. We hold his unwavering attention.

So if somebody chooses to ignore God, to turn away from him, to treat him like a switch that they can turn off, does his heart explode? When one of his handmade creations reaches the end of their life, does he yell "THAT'S MY CHILD!" as the last chance for relationship together slips away?

We neuter God of emotion too casually. Peter and Paul both wrote that God wants all people to be saved, that he doesn't want anyone to perish.[8] I've been in church long enough to not really think of what some words mean, so I looked it up. Perish. Suffer complete ruin or destruction.

Will everyone "make it"? I wish, but no. But we say that so offhandedly, as if real people aren't involved in the theological realities of sin, separation, helplessness, and the innate desire to search for rescue when they're sinking. We need to let emotions seep into our theological beliefs. Think of how God must feel when he looks at somebody who has no chance of their spiritual condition being helped, yet he *made* that person. Does he yell, "That's my child!"

The next twenty-four hours was my first time in a hospital. I remember holding Kath's hand while she was in a blue hospital gown. I remember the anesthesiologist. I remember kissing Kath before she was rolled away. And then sitting alone.

When we got back to Kath's folks that night, we put her in bed. I left the house. I walked for hours around the neighborhood numb, angry, confused, scared, sad. I yelled. I cried. I hurt.

Is that how Jesus felt looking at the crowds?

~~~

Compassion is an intense word. It's more emotional than concern and more personally disruptive than sympathy because it draws us toward an action. It's a deep love combined with an extreme desire to help a person and an aching until their situation changes; the kind of aching that keeps you up at night, consumes your thoughts, and affects your actions. There's an air of urgency that envelopes you – that something must be done and if that something fails, try again, and again, and again if needed.

Jesus saw the crowds, harassed and helpless, clueless and vulnerable, like sheep without a shepherd. And he had compassion for them. Literally the word means he was so emotionally hurting for them that his insides were in constant intense agony.

I have to admit I don't have that level of compassion, and if I'm honest and not hyper-spiritual about it, I probably never will. But I have learned something about myself. I become more like people that I spend time with. Have I become more like Jesus, feeling closer to how he did when he saw people?

~~~

I would do anything for my two girls. I think one of the worst feelings in the world would be if either of them was in trouble and there was absolutely nothing I could do to help them. I would go into a rage of emotions – helplessness, anger, rescue mode, fear, wanting to hold them and say "It's all right, I'm here," but unable to do it.

This is my bond with Jairus.[9] His daughter is dying. He's been to doctors and they can't cure her. He's been to the Temple, but he's not seeing his prayers answered. He has sat by her bed for endless hours, night after night, staring at her in the dark, haunted by the words floating in his mind. "What else can I do?...I don't know…" His only child. Twelve years old. Dying.

Jesus comes to town. He's very popular and a large crowd gathers. We don't know if that's fifty people, a hundred, five hundred, more, less, but it's a bunch of people around Jesus. I imagine everybody there is pushing to get closer to him. That's what you want to do around somebody famous, get close to them.

Suddenly Jairus comes, pushing and weaving his way through. But there's a distinct difference in Jairus' aggressiveness. Head rising above the crowd, fervent eyes searching wildly. "Let me through!" – more a command than a request. A man obsessed with a mission. After doubting for so long as to who Jesus is, after mounting intellectual and theological claims with other religious leaders to undermine Jesus, Jairus has reached a place deep inside that compels a respected synagogue leader to rush to Jesus. But the crowd doesn't see a synagogue leader. They see a father obsessed by desperate love for his daughter, pushing his way deeper into the crowd, driven by the belief that Jesus can heal her. He will *not* let a crowd of people stop him from getting to Jesus.

He falls at Jesus' feet. "My little girl is going to die! She's going to…die. Please come! Touch her! Do something so she can live. Just, please…" Jesus starts to his house.

But before they go far, a quiet almost whispered message is spoken into Jairus' ear. "Sir, your daughter…she has died. There's no use in bothering the Teacher now. Here, let us take you home."

I've tried to put myself in Jairus' place. I don't know how I would react. Hope in what could have happened is now useless. Silence. The unmoving bodies of the crowd. Dozens of heads bowing awkwardly, people not sure how to respond. Uncertainty in a father's voice. "What? No. That, that can't be true. She was just…I was…no…"

Low murmurs begin moving through the crowd. It builds to a constant background noise Jairus can't miss hearing. "Jairus' daughter is dead…She's dead…She's dead…" Unending, the words spread through the crowd. "She's dead…she's dead…" It surrounds the father while he's standing in the middle of the crowd. Hands touch his arms as he's covering his face. "Come on. We'll take you to her." There's an unintentional message they are implying here. Jesus is only a teacher. Death marks the limit of whatever power he might have.[10]

Then Jairus hears an interruption in the whispered buzzing. Different sound, different words. Not yelled over the noise in the street. Just spoken to him. "Don't be afraid. Just keep believing." Jairus' world stops for an ever so brief second – the calm voice of Jesus has spoken; the murmuring crowd, the echoing message from his home, all of it pauses. *Can I?*

One of the most powerful words in the English language might be *perhaps*. It communicates optimism and hopefulness. One of the most deflating words might be *maybe*. It's still hopeful, but much more uncertainty comes with it. They are almost identical words with little discernible difference except for the mood they communicate. Perhaps is to dream of trying. Maybe is to dream of something, then be stopped short. If one of my kids asks me to do something and I say "Maybe," they know it's pretty unlikely to happen and they'll walk away muttering, "Well, that means no."

Jairus chose the hope of *perhaps* to what Jesus said.

The funeral music can be heard before they arrive at his house. Jairus chose perhaps. *"Keep believing…"*

Jairus leads Jesus into his house, only to see it is already filled with people crying and weeping, bobbing up and down in mournful wails. *"Perhaps. I will keep believing…"*

Then Jesus says something that sounds completely idiotic to everybody present. "Stop all this crying! The girl isn't dead, only asleep." And people start *laughing* at him. It was obvious to everybody that she was dead! This teacher may know his Law and Prophets, but he doesn't know real life very well. When there's no heartbeat, no pulse, no breath, there's no life. Sorry, rabbi, but you're wrong.

I imagine Jairus standing by the door, Jesus beside him, his house filled with people, silently hanging onto one idea. *"...perhaps..."*

Jesus makes everybody leave the house. There are a few stares questioning his sanity, some derisively looking him up and down at the insensitivity to the family's situation. People convinced of something don't leave quietly. They make sure they get the last word in, even if it's said under their breath as they leave. "Hmph...she's dead".

"...perhaps..."

Jesus walks to the girl, holds her hand, and simply speaks. He doesn't ask anything. He doesn't tell Peter to get warm water and a towel. He doesn't talk to Jairus or his wife. He simply speaks. "Talitha koum." Little girl, get up. Stop being dead.

How often do I see dead things when what Jesus sees are things simply asleep?

There was no mistaking the physical condition of Jairus' daughter. She was dead. Did Jesus get it wrong then? "Oops. You're right. Sorry, my mistake."

In my eyes, from my perspective, there are so many dead things. That neighbor who has no interest in Jesus. The guy at work whose life is all about gaining more, making more, and being more. The brother who accepts the drug of "spirituality" that numbs him from looking deeper inside at the gaping holes in his life. The angry spouse who wants nothing to do with "church". The child who goes to college but seems to have left her faith at home. You may feel our government is dead, our school systems are dead, your dorm is dead. Some people say there are whole countries spiritually dead.

But in Jesus' divine perspective, perhaps they are just asleep. I can't explain how that works. Maybe it's impossible to explain the thought process of Christ. Maybe I don't have to. Maybe I need to be like Jairus, holding onto the "...perhaps..."

This has nothing to do with Jesus' ability to raise his daughter. It has to do with Jairus' relationship with God. Jesus could have proven he was more than just a teacher and indeed could heal by simply speaking a few words from back in town miles away and the girl would've been brought back to life.

But Jesus didn't. It could not have been easy. Jairus had to put aside what he was able to see. He had to put aside fear. He had to put aside what other people thought. He had to hold onto a father's hope. He had to wrestle with "Who do I really believe God is?" and then keep walking with the hope of perhaps.

Compassion is different from sympathy. Compassion sees hard, impossible situations and holds onto hope that something real has the power to intervene to rescue a person, to see things put right, even if it requires an awesome cost. Sympathy mourns a loss and comes beside the hurting person to help them let go of their dreams, to help bring closure and settle into a new reality.

Jesus saw the crowds standing in the middle of being harassed and helpless and felt compassion for each and every person, not sympathy. "That's my child! And I will *not* give up on him!"

The gospel writer Mark includes one more detail inside Jairus' house that gives us an intimate glimpse into God's heart. The exact words Jesus spoke. They aren't recorded in Greek like the rest of what Mark wrote. Just this one sentence is written in the everyday language of Aramaic, the common language used on the street, in the market, in the home, with family. They are the ordinary words used by every father who would wake up a sleeping child on any morning. *Talitha koum.* "Time to get up, little girl!"[11]

Do I feel with the same compassion and hope that Jesus felt for people – for my family, my neighbors, my kids' schools, my college, my city, other countries to hear those same words today?[12] "Time to get up, little girl."

Will I pray as Jesus prayed?

I believe the number one reason people don't do something is that they were never invited in the first place. There is a difference between inviting and announcing. So many times we hear announcements about opportunities in our church or schools or community; but a request to everybody is an invitation to nobody. An invitation is specifically directed towards me and has specific details intended to catch my attention.

Jesus is around crowds of hurting people. His followers have been watching, taking in the teaching and change that is happening in town after town, home after home. At night they likely talk between themselves trying to piece together what they were experiencing, asking Jesus questions, listening to him explain. Being with Jesus was changing them. So Jesus took them deeper and personally asked them to pray for something.

That alone should catch our attention and abruptly give us pause. This is *God* asking *us* to pray for something. Whatever that is should intensify, electrify, and jump out of our Bibles with two hands grabbing the sides of our head and shake us a bit to get our attention.

And Jesus says, "Ask the Lord of the harvest to send out workers into his harvest field."

Jesus doesn't tell his followers to pray for fruit or responsive hearts. They've already seen those exist. God is doing that. People are ready. God has already been at work long before anybody showed up. Jesus' prayer request seems benign and simple. He asks them to pray for laborers to harvest what God takes responsibility for growing.

~~~

It wasn't like this should have caught Jesus' followers off guard. Everything he did as he went through the villages and towns circled around this purpose: restore people to their right relationships, starting with their relationship with God. He couldn't stop talking about it.

Jesus did many things. Healing lepers, the blind, and crippled. Feeding thousands. Raising dead people. Walking on water. Stopping storms. Restoring dignity to prostitutes. Turning water into wine. Speaking to a fig tree so that it dies. But Jesus wasn't killed for any of these. Why kill a man who is feeding people? Doctors who might have lost patients to a traveling healer weren't the ones who took Jesus to the governor for execution. It wasn't pimps losing their women, vineyard owners losing business, or fig farmers who were afraid their crops would shrivel up. Something Jesus said or did clearly threatened some people. And it must have been something repeated often, otherwise it would have been dismissed as an off-hand comment. But Jesus' words are hard to dismiss.

It's said that every good speaker has one main message that he just packages differently. He speaks out of a passion, commitment, and knowledge of it. It's his priority. You see it when he's at the podium, hear it in his voice. You can tell he's going off script and going on heart. He sounds less like he's thinking and more like he's emoting. His body language is more fluid as his hands, steps, eyes, and head nods become extensions of the varying tones, volume, and flow of his words. Then he catches himself and says, "I'm sorry. Now where was I..." which we all take as an apology but if we're honest, we loved hearing several minutes of his passionate candor. *That's* what the speaker is about.

There are key times when you circle around to your primary drumbeat and passion. Jesus did the same.

Jesus' answer when asked why he came: "The Son of Man came not to be served but to serve others and to give his life as a ransom for many."[13] A ransom is paid by someone who values a kidnapped person in order to restore a *relationship* that has been broken. That relationship is more important than any ransom price paid.

Jesus describing God's love for people: "God so loved the world that…" what? That his very top priority was to feed it, get rid of cancer, fix global warming, end racism, or ensure everybody has an education? These are undeniably important and God aches that they exist, but he went bigger. "…that he gave his one and only Son so that everyone who believes in him will not perish but have eternal life."[14] What's eternal life? "And this is the real and eternal life: That they know you, the one and only true God, and Jesus Christ, whom you sent."[15] *Relationship.*

Jesus describing himself: "I am the good shepherd… I sacrifice my life for the sheep. I have other sheep, too, that are not in this sheepfold. I must bring them also. They will listen to my voice, and there will be one flock with one shepherd."[16] Jesus isn't content with having a good sized flock and taking care of just them. He's also focused on those who are *not* a part of the flock yet. *Sheep and shepherd have a relationship.*

In Luke 15, Jesus shares back-to-back-to-back story illustrations about something being lost – a sheep, a coin worth a day's earnings, and a son – all passionately looked for with every bit of focus and relentless pursuit, and after using all means available, is wildly celebrated when it is restored to the *relationship* it was supposed to be in all along. In these stories, none of the ones who lost the object ever said "It's just one. Let it go. The other ones are enough to have."

In times long ago, cadences – drums, chants, songs – were used to keep a continual pace while armies marched, farmers harvested, or pilgrims journeyed. It was the constant backdrop of their day. On page one of the Bible, God created a world in which we would have an indescribably intimate relationship with him, but Adam and Eve broke that relationship by disobedience. The next day God entered the garden. "Where are you?" he called to them. The drumbeat began. "Where are you?..." It was carried throughout the Old Testament. Jesus brought it to life. And today God continues intently seeking us with that same cadence.

"Where are you?...Where are you?...Where are you?..."

It's the emotionally charged obsessed passion of somebody searching. Like the man walking the hills looking for his sheep, like the woman looking in every crevice of her house for her coin, like a father sitting outside his door staring down the path each day for years looking for his son to come home, God bears the aching of waiting for an answer back. "Where are you?..." He cares *passionately* about us!

And that is why Jesus asks his followers to pray for people to be laborers as God is calling out. But there's an intense risk in praying as Jesus prayed. To honestly pray it, the disciples would have to wrestle with a question God would be asking: "What if I want you to be the answer to your own prayers, what would you do?" This question God poses to us is invasive, inconvenient, and irresistible.

The sending out of workers and laborers is so important that the One in charge of the harvest doesn't entrust how it will be done to anybody except himself. Jesus' request isn't for workers to just go wandering aimlessly into the field. His request is specific. "Ask the

Lord of the harvest…" – the one who has the highest-vested interest in the success of the harvest – "to send out workers," to go where He sees they are most needed, not necessarily where they may want to naturally go. Send implies they go somewhere other than where they are at this time. Jesus disturbingly and disruptively does not say "Ask the Lord of the harvest to keep workers right here."

He also sends them out with a clear, distinct, understood purpose of what their task is – and that task may not align with their wants and needs, but it will align with God's.

~~~

Each year on the first day of pre-season training, legendary football coach Vince Lombardi would gather all his players together. This team meeting was required no matter if you were a rookie or a veteran player. As Lombardi walked to the front of the room, he would silently look over the men for several seconds until he had their complete attention. They might have been promising rookies or returning stars whose names were known around the country, but he was the unquestionable boss.

Lombardi would hold up a pigskin and say five words. "Gentlemen, this is a football," and then explain how this was the most important object in the game. Then he would march them out to the field and have them stand in the end zone, where he would say, "And this is the only place the football needs to get to."

Why do this each year? Why do this to men who had been playing the game since they were ten years old and knew what a football was and where it was supposed to go? Repetition. And necessity. 'Gentlemen, we're going to start with the basics and make sure the fundamental things are executed well. And in case you forget, I'll tell you again and again and again.'

What were Jesus' *first words* to the first followers he found, fishermen tossing fishing nets? "Come, follow me, and I will show you how to fish for people!"[17]

What was Jesus' *last prayer* to God for his followers? "Just as you sent me into the world, I am sending them into the world."[18]

What did Jesus promise his closest followers *after his resurrection*? "But you will receive power when the Holy Spirit comes upon you. And you will be my witnesses, telling people about me everywhere – in Jerusalem, throughout Judea, in Samaria, and to the ends of the earth."[19]

What were Jesus' *last words* his followers heard from him? "I have been given all authority in heaven and on earth…" They had just spent forty days with Jesus after he was killed, so the question of having authority would have been kind of hard to argue against, but Jesus makes it clear. He has the authority to say what he said next. When I really want to get a point across to my kids, I start off saying, "All right, everybody, *listen up!*" and they know I'm dead serious. If what Jesus just said is true, if a person saying they are a follower of Jesus really believes that he has all authority, then you know the next words out of his mouth are of the utmost importance. "…therefore, go and make disciples of all nations [or peoples]."[20] This has become known as the Great Commission.

"Gentlemen, this is my kingdom. This is how this game is played. This is how this game is won. This is what *you* are supposed to do." If Jesus chose to keep repeating this to the people closest to him at the key moments of their journey together, it must have been a basic fundamental task that comes with being a follower of Christ.

~~~

Does this mean that everybody will hear "Where are you?" and respond "Here!"? I wish this were true, but no. Jesus' own ministry shows this. How many hundreds of people saw what he did to reinforce his spoken kingdom message and they still walked away, ignoring him or turning on him, and in the end only a few embracing him?[21]

Arthur Glasser, who was a missionary to China before being a longtime seminary professor, wrote "There is more willingness on God's part to save sinners than there is on the part of sinners to be saved. And there is more grace to

give than there are hearts willing to receive it."[22] Jesus tells
a story about this, how much God wants his people, but
not all will want him. A great banquet is given by an
incredibly rich man. He sends his servant out to personally
invite people. "Come on, everything is ready and waiting
for you! My master is eager to have you!" But people
apologize and have their reasons for not coming. Too
many things are happening in their lives to make this feast
stand out; other things supersede his generosity. No
amount of passionate inviting sways them.

The master is outraged, so he sends his servant out to
the roads and fields to find anybody who needs a meal.
"But, sir, there's still room." "Then go find more! Go
everywhere you can! I want my house full!"[23]

So exactly how will this invitation, this gospel, get to
those people? "Follow me and I will make you fishers of
men." "As you sent me, I am sending them." "Go and
make disciples of all nations." "You will be my witnesses
in…" "Ask the Lord of the harvest to send out
workers…"

~~~

But it is a risk to pray as Jesus prayed and heed his
response, which may mean being willing to be an answer
to our own prayers. It's easy to say that fear will not stop
me when nothing is threatening my safe world and I can
wax philosophically about the drive of inner man to

achieve great things regardless of the cost and obstacles. "Damn the torpedoes, full speed ahead!"

But Jesus didn't send out people with false bravado. On the contrary, he was pretty clear of what they should expect. Jesus' invitation should have brought some fear. "I am sending you out like sheep among wolves."[24] As one man who has lived in spiritually difficult countries wrote, "To me, the most startling thing Jesus ever said was when He assigned His followers the task of going out in pairs to share His gospel news with lost people. He said that He was sending them 'as sheep among wolves.' Still, He expected them to prevail. In the history of the world, no sheep has ever won a fight with a wolf. The very idea is insane."[25]

We are not called to be stupidly risky for Christ, but we are called to be radical stewards which will require releasing the anchors that hold us in place and knowingly drift into the unknown. That requires risk. In one of the parables that Jesus told, a rich man gives servants different amounts of money to take care of while he is on a journey. None of the servants are treated exactly alike. One gets five bags of gold, another three bags, another one bag. Each has different abilities and so are supplied differently. But the expectation is that all of them would use, take advantage of, and handle the responsibility for which they have been entrusted. Two know that for this to happen it will involve stepping into risk and then acting on that risk. The third considers the risk too great and does nothing, afraid of what could happen. When the rich man returns, each man has to report how he stewarded the opportunity and trust.[26]

I guess for each of those servants, and for me, the situation could be written up like this mathematical expression. Which is greater –

embrace opportunity $> ? <$ fear repercussions

~~~

I desperately want this God story to be true and believe it is true, but I'm afraid a time will come when I'll get comfortable and settle for it to be true from a distance, like how I experience war through movies. Dirt exploding and patriotism and heroic stands and bad guys being defeated, but it's always other people experiencing it. I have no idea what war is. Battles become pictures, removed, distant to me. Some people die, some people live, and that's my understanding of war. Roll movie credits. I can do the same, be lulled into a lethargic stupor with this mission Jesus gave and simply watch from a distance rather than accept his invitation to get in the dirt with him.

The men and women that made up the first churches, the people of today creating ministry presences in small remote villages, and the Christ followers choosing to live in our urban areas, know following Jesus has complexity and layers and emotions. It isn't just 'Let's talk about the Jesus I know' in a utopian experience. Following Jesus with his priorities also means pain and fear and exhilaration and mystery and confrontation and fun and choices and indecision and breathtaking experiences and gut wrenching loss and camaraderie and loneliness and knowing and not knowing and victory and death. It's real.

I don't want to be numb. I need to be reminded that this God Story is real, not some general philosophical point of discussion or contemplation that happens "out there" with some nameless "them" doing it. I want to feel cheated if I'm missing out.

~~~

There's a surprising almost footnote-like ending to the story of the prodigal son in Luke 15. Remember that Jesus has just given three stories (about a lost sheep, a coin, and a son) following the same pattern – something is missing, it is searched for, it is restored, then there is ridiculous celebration. But after he shares these short stories, Jesus tacks on an extra bit to the last one, the one about the lost son. He briefly tells us how the other brother complains to his father that he's been the faithful son but has never been thrown such an extravagant party.

I wonder, during all those years of being the good son and enjoying the benefits of his father's household, did he ever talk about his brother? Did he ever ask his father about the hurt, pain, or longing the man must have felt, trying to understand the aching? Did his younger brother's absence from where he should be ever gnaw at him? Did he ever get up before the meal was done and say "This isn't right! I'm going to go find him and bring him home!" Did he ever stand by the road looking down it with his father?

Or was his missing brother always "that other son of yours" who was gone somewhere doing something and it would be nice if he showed up someday maybe? The way the older brother reacted when this did come true answers these questions for me.

I don't want to become numb to missing people who aren't where they are supposed to be. Henry Blackaby wrote in *Experiencing God*, "You may be called upon to attempt things only God can do, where formerly you may have attempted only that which you knew you could do."[27] I don't need to be God. I just need to be willing to be an answer to a prayer Jesus asks us to pray – to send out workers into God's field that is ready. And accept that this is a personally risky prayer.

Will I do as Jesus did? (Who, *me?*)

Before the adventures began for the group that would forever be known as the Fellowship of the Ring, Frodo Baggins lived quietly in the Shire. He tended his gardens, his kitchen, his books, and his pipe the same way that any respectable hobbit would. But he was a bit odd compared to the rest. He always seemed to others to be discontent, though nobody really knew why, even Frodo himself. Some hobbits said this was because of his very close relationship with that uncle of his, Bilbo, who told tales of a grand adventure he had been on. Quirky fellow. Who would want to go beyond the border of home, the Shire?

But now we are in Frodo's home. A fire is lit. Pipe smoke fills the room. Gandalf the Gray sits. He has just told Frodo about the Ring of Power, the one ring that will give the evil Sauron control over all Middle Earth, unless the ring is destroyed. That same ring which sits in Frodo's jacket pocket on a chain, left for him by Bilbo.

"I do really wish to destroy it!" cried Frodo. "Or, well, to have it destroyed. I am not made for perilous quests. I wish I had never seen the Ring! Why did it come to me? Why was I chosen?"

"Such questions cannot be answered," said Gandalf. "You may be sure it was not for any merit that others do not possess; nor for power or wisdom. But you have been chosen, and you must therefore use such strength and heart and wits as you have."[28]

The early church, Christians today, and those who will follow after us will all relate with the tension Frodo feels. The idyllic world we convince ourselves we live in has been disturbed by the weight of what we now know and see around us – the harassed and helpless in our towns and cities, our universities, other countries – if only we look past our safe Christian and church borders. We really do want to do something, but we cannot grasp what, or why, God would ask us to undertake something that we cannot possibly accomplish. There's a dissonance that comes upon us once we possess awareness and explanations of things. What had been only a ring on a chain now is a responsibility to carry out.

How can we possibly ever do as Jesus did?! Our western strategic-thinking, goal-oriented, achievement-focused minds need to slow down a bit and ask this question: How does Jesus assume we will be able to do what he did given who we are?

Let's be honest. There's something inside us that wants to be a hero. We want to be in the action, taking risks, being heroes.

Blake Snyder, a Hollywood screenwriter, in his book *Save The Cat!,* lists the ten basic storylines in which all

movies fit. One he calls "Dude With A Problem."[29] An
ordinary guy is having an ordinary day when something
extraordinarily bad enters it. He must dig deep inside to
defeat it, taking some hits along the way. "Little guy has
big huge problems and stands up to big bad guy and
defeats him" is Tolkien's Lord of The Rings trilogy, all the
Star Wars movies, Indiana Jones' life story, every John
Wayne movie, movies about prisoners of war struggling to
survive, most movies about the small guy taking on big
government, the story of David and Goliath, Moses and
Pharaoh, even Jairus and his dying daughter. We consider
ourselves to be ordinary just like these people and get
drawn into their story, rooting for the little guy.

Sometimes when I'm mindlessly mowing the yard I
catch myself daydreaming about the great risks I'd take to
protect my family if our house was attacked by terrorists
(although I don't ever really come up with a good reason
why terrorists would come to our house in the first place).
I always get shot a few times and my body is in terrible
pain, doubtful I'll even survive, but I've taken out the well-
armed, highly-trained bad guys with my quick reflexes and
superior intellect and saved the day. Then my mower hits a
thick clump of grass and *kachunk* the engine stops and I'm
back to plain old me.

Ordinary.

Frodo has to enter Mordor with only Sam and bipolar
Sméagol. The Empire has Darth Vader, a bazillion
Stormtroopers, and a planet-sized laser; Luke has…two

droids and an old light saber. The German army is more powerful than Indiana Jones. The banditos have more guns than The Duke. Everybody breaks in Japanese POW camps. David is smaller than Goliath. Dead girls don't come back to life.

There's an event recorded in Acts 4 that we would do well to take a walk through. Peter and John are in Jerusalem. It's three in the afternoon, time for prayer, and they walk with the flow of Jews towards the Temple gates. No different than any other day. For hundreds of people, this was the normal routine.

Even the lame man on the steps didn't change. Each day his friends carried him there and then they would come back to take him home at sunset. He sat there, begging, waiting for somebody to drop a coin or two in his hand as an act of charity. People would be more motivated to help the poor and destitute right in front of the Almighty's Temple. "Help a cripple…help a cripple…" with his hand out, his eyes looking up but not really looking at anything. After all, this was routine too.

Peter and John approach the entrance, then stop. Why this particular time as opposed to the hundreds of others they had passed by this same spot, this same man, we don't know. This time, though, they stopped.

And they looked at him very intently. This isn't one of the normal passer-by glances out of the corner of your eye, or a causal courteous "How are you doing?" communicated by a head nod. They see him, really see him, see him as Jesus saw him. They see a person, not a cripple.

But the man just continues sitting there with his hand out.

"Look at us!" Peter says. The man looks up, maybe blinks a bit, expecting some money. Nobody ever stopped to *talk* to unclean cripples on their way to prayer. He was used to looking away when people approached him. He was dirty, outcast, different. Subhuman, people would say. But these men wanted the outsider's eyes towards them. So he looks up. *Maybe some coins…*

"In the name of Jesus Christ of Nazareth, get up and walk!" The man doesn't know what to do.

So Peter takes his hand – in front of a crowd, in front of the Temple, he touches an unclean man! – and helps him. And the man stands…then walks…then jumps! He talks loudly, praising God, then in silent shock, shakes his head trying to understand, then is overwhelmed again and shouts more praises to God. People see this and at first probably think it's irreverent to carry on in such a way in front of the Lord's House. But then word starts spreading. "That's the lame man…" People are thunderstruck and start rushing to the gate, finding the man holding tightly onto Peter and John, his legs unable to stay still.

Then Peter speaks. "People, what is so surprising about this? Why are you staring at us? Isn't it God – the God of our fathers – who has brought glory to his servant Jesus by doing this?…" He goes on to remind all who are listening that he's talking about the same Jesus that they had just weeks before killed, but God raised from the dead. "And we are witnesses of this fact!"

Peter continues. Priests come out of the Temple and are very uneasy. Soon they call the Temple guard and arrest the two men for talking about a risen-from-the-dead Jesus.

The next morning Peter and John are brought before the whole council of Jewish rulers, which includes some of the very same men who had brought charges to Pontius Pilate and demanded that Jesus be crucified. "By what power and in whose name have you done this?"

Then Peter, filled with the Holy Spirit, said to them, "Rulers and elders of our people, are we being questioned today because we've done a good deed to a crippled man? Do you want to know how he was healed? Let me clearly state to all of you and to all the people that he was healed by the powerful name of Jesus Christ, the man you crucified but whom God raised from the dead...There is salvation in no one else! God has given no other name under heaven by which we must be saved!" If it were possible to have at the exact same moment a sense of awed quiet and angry outburst ready to erupt in the same room, this was such a time.

Yet the writer of this account draws attention to something that was even more strongly present, describing the scene this way: "When they saw the courage of Peter and John and realized that they were unschooled, ordinary men, they were astonished and took note that these men had been with Jesus."[30]

These extremely ordinary men saw extraordinary things happen as a direct overflow of their relationship with God. There are several things the verse did *not* say. It doesn't say they stood out because of their academic acumen (quite the opposite was true) or their synagogue certification or their stage presence or voice projection or ability to handle the scriptures with confidence. All of these are good and would aid in any ministry, but it wasn't what made them stand out before the community. They had simply been with Jesus. It does make you wonder what the leaders actually *saw* in Peter and John that made them draw that conclusion. Somehow in the events of the previous twenty-four hours, these two ordinary men's actions and words brought back echoes of a man this same group of leaders had crucified just weeks before. They thought they had rid themselves of this troublemaker, and now they were seeing his presence and priorities live on. Jesus had rubbed off on his followers.

One of these two men, John, captured this idea for us, writing down something Jesus had told his followers the night he was betrayed. "I am the vine, you are the branches. People who remain in me, and I in them, are the ones who bear plenty of fruit. Without me, you see, you can't do anything."[31] We can't do anything for God, value what God values, or take on his character, passions, loves, or priorities without being connected to God first. You become like those you spend time with.

The longer I've looked at the ordinary people in the Bible and have spent time with ordinary men and women around the world who are serving God in his field, I begin to see they all have a vine-branch relationship with him. The bigger the problem they faced, the greater the odds they had to overcome and the more dependent on the vine they became. You can't have courage in the absence of something to fear, and you won't have courage unless you have something to hold onto. When these men and women dug down deep inside, they grabbed ahold of something that let them handle the big problems they faced. And the very person they held onto, Jesus, gave them the strength to walk and act as Jesus himself did.

One of our former pastors wrote *The Four Spiritual Secrets* which came from his desire to live out this relationship of the vine and its branches. Until his death at age eighty-three, Dick Woodward would tell people that the best ministry days he had were the decades when he was confined to bed because of a degenerative disease that left him a quadriplegic. If anyone needed to ask "Who, me? What can I do?" it was Dick Woodward, but instead he lived out John 15.

Over the years I have shared his Four Secrets with people who feel something about who they are – an abuse or addiction or choice they regret in their past, a fear, a lack of a skill, an illness, their skin color, no seminary training, a stuttering problem – would keep them from being useable by God in what God is doing. Dick summed up John 15 in this way:

> I'm not, but He is.
> And I am in Him, and He is in me.
>
> I can't, but He can.
> And I am in Him, and He is in me.
>
> I don't want to, but He wants to.
> And I am in Him, and He is in me.
>
> I didn't, but He did.
> Because I was in Him, and He was in me.

<u>One day in a village with Jesus</u>

Most songs follow a basic pattern. There's a verse and a chorus, a second verse and the chorus again, and then a third verse and the chorus. But then there might be this slightly different part, the bridge. The rhythm might change a bit; the words sound similar, but also different. The bridge has a purpose. We the listener are supposed to slow down, reflect a minute on what has already been heard, and prepare for the climax where the song's main theme is picked up again with the final verse and chorus.

This short chapter is our bridge.

Pause. Before going any further, I want us to stop and ask a question.

"Is all of this so far a good summary of the ideas and values Jesus talked about, or does it also have actual substance backing it up?" Jesus was a masterful storyteller and had an unparalleled ability to ask penetrating questions, but isn't Matthew 9:35-38 ("Jesus went throughout all the towns and villages…") just a summary that can make a good preaching outline? See as Jesus saw. Feel as Jesus felt. Pray as Jesus prayed. Did Matthew record for us simply the easily talked about philosophy behind Jesus' words, or were they a real part of Jesus' ministry? Each of Jesus' disciples had to draw their own conclusions, and they had roughly a thousand days with him to do so.

Each encounter with Jesus was a pulsating story. It always had a seeker and a rescuer and usually some confrontation or doubter on the sidelines. It frequently ended in amazement for whoever was present. Jesus' closest followers got to see this over and over and over. It had to leave an impression. For them, each village they entered brought a question. "If I go down this road, where is he taking me? What lies around the bend?" both literally and figuratively. Their understanding of "normal" would be shaken. They would not be the same.

Each day brought a new experience…

~~~

When Jesus arrived in Capernaum, the town started buzzing. From the air, the house he is in looks like an anthill, people coming down different paths and walkways toward the front door. They have come to see Jesus, each with his own reason. Curious. Antagonistic. Hopeful. Hurt.

Jesus is in this house teaching people. The room is crowded. There are the normal background noises, odors, and movements that you have when you gather dozens of people together in a one-room house.

And Jesus is teaching them God's Word. We don't know exactly what, but it is something that is keeping the crowd's attention. Religious leaders stand by the walls, distrustful skeptics. More people are trying to squeeze into the doorway or find a small line of sight through the window.

Then – *crack, crash!* – the ceiling starts falling apart! Was it a mud ceiling being chipped through, or a tile roof being removed, or a wood one where branches were being snapped? I don't know. All I know is that whatever it was, it started falling down on people's heads.

And Jesus stays put. He doesn't leave. He doesn't complain. He isn't telling whoever is above his head that their timing is terribly rude and to come back later when he's done teaching. He's not even trying to get the crowd's attention back on him instead of on the hole forming above. He's just waiting. Maybe a minute, maybe just fifteen seconds. Have you ever sat patiently for fifteen seconds in the midst of sudden interruptions? It goes on forever.

In the midst of people's shouts and scattering to not be hit by falling debris, a hole at least five feet wide opens up. The hole has to be that big because all of a sudden a mat is lowered down, a mat with a man on it, a man who can't move. Paralyzed.[32]

~~~

[This next section is a fictitious narrative. I've read several commentaries to try to get a sense of what a paralytic's life was like. A narrative seemed like a good way to share it.]

Capernaum, the day before.

The man is laying in his own filth.

The road is a constant motion of people in the morning hours, but the man has spent so many hours over the years watching them walk by that there is little body language he misses, especially the subtle snubs of people pretending not to notice him. A slight slowing in their step when the odor hits them. The pause in conversation when they see his soiled and stained clothing and the quick look in the other direction so they don't make eye contact. Then the small sidestep as they walk past, trying to put a little more space between themselves and the man.

What do they think I'm going to do, the man thought. *Throw myself on them? Now that would be funny. An invalid covered in pee, filth, and flies flopping across the road. Some old lady would think Satan himself was after her!* The man can't help letting a quiet smirking "hmph" come out, just as a woman and her daughter are passing by. They jump and sidestep.

For two centuries fishing has defined Capernaum. Fleets of fishing boats come and go on the Sea of Galilee, great crowds fill the market places daily. There are more than a dozen fishing villages on the shores of the lake, but none of them busier than Capernaum. Everywhere men and women are haggling over the price of the freshest fish to take home. Men with calloused hands grab fish, tossing them into piles. The fishermen are exhausted from hours of throwing their nets into the water and then hauling them in; but now they must repair their nets, preparing for tonight's fishing.

The man's mind doesn't take in any of the sounds or sights. Not that he's unable to, but when your day is spent laying against a wall watching, you can only care so much about what is happening in the lives of those who walk by.

*Walking. I would give anything to do that...*he tries to stop these thoughts. They're like scratching at a scab. You know you shouldn't, but you can't stop even though you know it will open up the wound to start bleeding again.

...Walking. Going places, anywhere. With people. Seeing things. Having a life. Being somebody. But why complain? I am somebody. I'm the man sitting in his own... Call it whatever you want – poop, filth, dung, excrement – but when you are sitting in it all day, feeling it seep through the fabric of your clothes, see it stain the ground around you, the stench hovering around you, "it" becomes part you.

A fisherman walks up the road and smells the odor. *Augh. How can that man stand himself? Even the flies from hell must be tortured to be near him.* The fisherman comes this way when he works the boats with his brother. He is always caught off guard as he leaves the salty smells of the fish and nets and comes up this road. He picks up his pace to get upwind.

As Peter takes a slight sidestep around the paralytic, the man pays no attention. He is familiar with the quickening of steps as people pass by. He is numb in his own thoughts. The scab has been scratched.[33]

[End of narrative.]

~~~

As the man is lowered into the house, Jesus looks up to the hole. Heads are peering over the edge, just a few feet above Jesus. Maybe they are lowering the mat on ropes and Jesus sees them feeding the line through their hands. Maybe they are close enough that the men on the roof just pick up the mat and put the paralyzed man through the hole and people inside instinctively reach up to grab hold and lower it. Regardless of how he got down, all three biblical reports of this story do say one thing, which must mean we're supposed to catch it. Jesus sees their faith. Not the paralyzed man's faith. His friends' faith.

And Jesus turns to the man on the mat laying there in front of him. Is the man looking up eagerly, quietly asking "Please, heal me"? Is he embarrassed, maybe hopeful earlier outside the house, but now feeling dozens of eyes on him? Is he angry, raging inside a self-imposed cage of self-pity at the four so-called friends who should have just left him alone to die since each day is another one of pain and loneliness? We are left in the dark.

Then Jesus completely invades the paralyzed man's thoughts. "My friend, your sins, all of them, are forgiven."

Tim Keller writes about this interaction:

Jesus is confronting the paralytic with his main problem by driving him deep. Jesus is saying, "By coming to me and asking for only your body to be healed, you're not going deep enough. You have underestimated the depths of your longings, the longings of your heart." ...[S]urely this man would have been resting all his hopes in the possibility of walking again. In his heart he's almost surely saying, "If only I could walk again, then I would be set for life. I'd never be unhappy, I would never complain. If only I could walk, then everything would be right." And Jesus is saying, "My son, you're mistaken." That may sound harsh, but it's profoundly true. Jesus says, "When I heal your body, if that's all I do, you'll feel you'll never be unhappy again. But wait two months, four months – the euphoria won't last. The roots of discontent of the human heart go deep."[34]

It takes a few seconds for Jesus' words to sink in. Seconds after Jesus talks forgiveness, people raise eyebrows in shock and alarm and even angry dismissal.

"Who is this man?" they critically ask themselves. "He's claiming to be God. Only God can forgive sins! This is blaspheme!"

Then the crowd hears Jesus ask a question. "Which is easier: to say to the paralytic, 'Your sins are forgiven,' or to say, 'Get up, take your mat, and walk'?"[35] It's obviously easier to *say* sins are forgiven because nobody can prove it. Anybody can *say* it, but it doesn't mean anything has happened. But which of the two would be easier to actually *accomplish*? People in the house were good, religious men and women who knew the spiritual eternal state of one's soul was much more significant than the use of legs during a lifetime. Forgiveness from God was obviously more important, and only God could accomplish that. But then again, only God could heal irreparable legs too. So the question is really rhetorical. Only God could do both.

So Jesus tells them all, "Just so it's clear that I'm the Son of Man and authorized to do either, or both..."[36] he turned to the man and said, "Get up, pick up your mat, and go home." The man jumped up, picked up his mat, and walked right out through the crowd! And everybody who saw this was absolutely amazed and said, "We have never seen anything like this!"

It seems cruel that Jesus didn't just go ahead and heal this man right away, or for that matter heal every sickness and even raise more people from the dead since he obviously had the power to, and did so more than once. [37] Jesus knew he could, but he was not sent to set up an emergency care center. He had a greater purpose. However, he showed his power to people, allowing them to see something they could verify – something tangible – in order that they might also have faith in the unbelievable and the unthinkable – that sins could really be forgiven.

~~~

The four know this man. He's not a social case or a project. He's their friend. They always wanted to do something for him, but the best they could do on any given day was try to get him something cleaner to wear, sit with him, be his friend. It was a risk though. Lame people were considered unclean. They were "un-whole" and unholy. People who had continual contact with them, even for good reasons, were considered to be snubbing the ordained order of things and were unclean in doing so.

But then these men heard Jesus was at a nearby house, a few streets and corners away. And they did what they could to get their friend there.

Evangelism is one of those words which everybody has their own reaction to. Some cringe in fear and do whatever they can to avoid it. Some see it as an uncomfortable obligation that we put off as much as possible, like doing our taxes or going to the dentist. Some see it as a drug that gives a rush. We all have our own images and definitions of evangelism, which affect how and if we "do" evangelism.

Can I give you my definition? Evangelism is simply trying to find ways to get my crippled friends in the house to meet Jesus. That's it.

If I care about this person enough, I will do whatever it takes to get him in the house to see Jesus. When the men were carrying their paralyzed friend to Jesus, the crowd in the roads and doorways didn't stop them. They didn't dejectedly say, "Oh, I'm so sorry, buddy, but we'll have to try another time." "Well, I guess we can pray for you." "Bummer, but at least we tried." No. They responded with action. "Hey, let's bust through the roof!" Genius!

I'm sure as they were making the hole, they weren't exactly being cheered on, especially by those inconvenienced below, but that didn't stop them. I imagine people are yelling at them, making demands to stop all this mess-making and interruption, and the four radiate determination you can see in their eyes that says, "No way! We can't stop! He's too important!" Jesus recognizes this bold love as an expression of faith. Their focus was simply on seeing their friend get to Jesus.

Then from the rooftop, leaning over a hole they had made, dust still settling, their friend lying motionless on a mat, a crowd of irritated and now dirty people making noise, they hear Jesus talking to their friend. Not yelling. Not making a scene. Just stating something to him. "My friend, your sins, all of them, are forgiven."

The four friends did their part. God did His.

Evangelism is not us making converts. No one has ever made someone else a believer in Jesus. We are called to evangelize, to help people be able to have the chance to hear about and meet Jesus; God is the one who meets the person heart-to-heart and changes or converts their thoughts and heart. The decision of faith is still the paralyzed man's, and every human being's. The faith and love in action of the friends brought this man to the source of his complete healing, but he still had to decide on his own ultimately. I may hold out $100 to somebody and say it's his, but until he actually takes it from me, it's not his possession. But I still need to make sure it's offered to him.

~~~

I was in West Africa under a mango tree sharing this same story with some believers. Most of us were talking about the different things we took from the story. One of the men, though, was sitting very quietly. He had one of those "I'm listening but not really listening to you; I'm wrestling in my mind" kind of looks on his face.

In the region I was in, there are very few Christians. The Muslim population doesn't kill or burn the houses of Christians, but they do make life very difficult for followers of Isa al-Mesih (Jesus the Messiah). Socially they are put outside of the community. If they own a shop, people will stop coming to it. Help isn't offered for planting or taking in crops. I thought Badu was thinking about this new definition of evangelism and how it would look in his community.

Finally, Badu stood. As one of the leaders of the small Christian community, what he says carries a lot of weight. I wasn't expecting what I heard.

"I am sorry. I have dishonored God. When this story was shared, my heart ached. I thought it was because our Muslim friends are like that paralyzed man. But God told me to listen to the story again. I thought of the four friends and Jesus, but God told me to keep listening. I thought of the religious leaders in the house watching this, but God told me to keep listening. Then I heard. And I saw myself in the story. And God said to me, 'Stop being part of the crowd!'"

Whenever we read stories in the Bible, we often forget the extras. We give them the same importance as the guys in movie credits who have minor roles. But God includes the details in each story for a reason, including the seemingly insignificant nameless character roles.

The crowd. What did they do to help the man? Nothing. They didn't clear a path so the paralyzed man could get to Jesus. They didn't help make a hole in the roof. The lack of mentioning them doing anything to actually help leads me to think they probably thought this interruption was exactly that, an interruption. After all, Jesus was teaching them! What could be more important than that?! So they stood there.

So often we read in the Bible about crowds of people wanting to be with Jesus but keeping those who needed Jesus the most away! Being part of the crowd following Jesus wasn't an exclusive, invitation only club, but crowds do often communicate to outsiders' subtle snubs or standards that can't be met. Or maybe they were trying to protect Jesus, as if they couldn't let him get dirty. Crowds tried to keep Bartimaeus, a blind man, away as he called out to Jesus. Zacchaeus, a very short man and a social outsider, found no opening made for him in a crowd of people who were watching Jesus walk down a road. A woman who had been sick for years had to sneak through the crowd just wanting to touch the edge of Jesus' clothes. A crowded house was listening to Jesus and not a single person said, "Hey, move aside and let these four guys through the door!" And each of these times Jesus stopped what he was doing.

Badu told us that he was so focused on helping other believers grow in a spiritually difficult area that he wasn't really looking around to see who among his Muslim neighbors were "wanting to get in the house to see Jesus".

We need to remember that ministry is God's gift to us, not our gift to God. He doesn't need us to decide when to bring somebody to him, which left to our own timing would be when it's convenient and not intrusive. Rather, he allows us to see him change a heart when that heart is ready to be changed.

Badu's comment brought an uncomfortably raw thought into my mind: Are we so successful in our churches and ministries and busy with our Christian lives that we don't have time for the intrusion of sinners meeting Jesus?

I confess that I am like the crowd too, preoccupied with my relationships, plans, and even ministry that I often am not even looking around me for people who are trying to get in the house to see Jesus.

Christopher Wright says in *The Mission of God*,

Fundamentally, our mission (if it is biblically informed and validated) means our committed participation as God's people, at God's invitation and command, in God's own mission within the history of God's world for the redemption of God's creation…Our mission flows from and participates in the mission of God.[38]

Will I do as Jesus did? (Do *what*?)

What Jesus did was very simple. He went. There's nothing deep, complex, or confusing about that. He simply went to people where they were. Good people, bad people, scared people, hurting people, proud people, angry people, searching people, alone people. And he talked about restoring them. "Turn from the things that are keeping you broken. Aren't you tired of coming up empty? The Kingdom – the very heart of what you've been looking for to fill those gaps and holes and echoing caverns in your life – is coming. It's time to make things right."

Jesus' followers must have been at times in wonder, and at other times silent, and still other times shell shocked as they saw the wide range of ways people responded. At the end of any given day I imagine them sitting on the ground outside a house eating bread and talking about the things they had seen since breakfast.

And lingering in the back of their minds was what Jesus had said. "Ask the Lord of the harvest to send out workers into his harvest field," with that unavoidable risk associated with it. *Will you be an answer to your own prayer?*

You're seeing what that looks like. My priorities aren't obscure. I'm inviting you to go there with me.

Therein lies the inconvenience of being discipled by Jesus, of becoming more like him, which John already summed up for us. "I am the vine, you are the branches. When you're joined with me and I with you...the harvest is sure to be abundant. Separated, you can't produce a thing."[39] That's obvious. Cut a branch off and it dries up and shrivels. It can't survive or grow or produce leaves or fruit unless it's connected. Branches are *supposed* to do these things. A branch on an apple tree grows apples, an orange tree oranges, a banana tree bananas. It's not complicated. There's a life-giving relationship between the tree and the branch, with the branch taking on the characteristics of the tree, not the opposite.

So it makes sense that Jesus was saying to his followers "If you are going to be connected to me, then you will have the same characteristics as me, including my priorities." We try to reverse it, but it simply doesn't work that way. An apple has never told the apple tree he wants things to change so he can become an orange. Jesus is saying "If you're genuinely in me and I'm in you then you *have* to be about what I'm about, because it doesn't work the other way."

In the Old Testament, God described the coming Messiah (who is Jesus) to Israel, the people of God, saying "It is *too small* a thing for you to be my servant to restore the tribes of Jacob and bring back those of Israel I have kept. I will *also* make you a light for the Gentiles, that you may bring my salvation to the ends of the earth."[40] It is by no means wrong to seek the spiritual development of those who are already "in the family" through personal growth and fellowship and worship. People assume there are sides to be taken between doing discipleship and doing missions, as if they are two separate parties competing for majority sway within the church. They are not! They make each other stronger, and neglecting one slowly chips away the strength of the other.

But we have a favored pull towards the more comfortable of the two. This is not enough for the mission of the Messiah in God's plan. Another version of Isaiah's words reads "But that's not a big enough job for my servant — just to recover the tribes of Jacob, merely to round up the strays of Israel. I'm setting you up as a light for the *nations* so that my salvation becomes *global!*"[41] So when Jesus is describing the vine-and-branches relationship, he reminds those listening, "*This* is what I'm about. So if you're in me and I'm in you and you want to be like me, then you have to go where I'm going and do what I'm doing. I can't be limited to things that are too small for what God's design is for me."

There's a lot more in Jesus saying "Come follow me"[42] than an invitation to just spending time together with him. It is an invitation to change your identity. David Platt wrote, "If our lives do not reflect the fruit of following Jesus, then we are foolish to think that we are actually followers of Jesus in the first place."[43]   This is the invitation of the vine, but we live in a culture with so much Christian noise that we can't hear it often or clearly.

~~~

Advertisers are determined to take every opportunity to get you to buy their product. They understand that most people are moved to buy what they are comfortable with. The more you see something, the more familiar it becomes, the more likely you are to consider buying it. My friend Rick worked for an ad agency in New York City twenty years ago. He said that a person needed to see a product ad at least twelve times before they were motivated enough to buy it. If that was the industry standard twenty years ago, I'd guess the number has only gone up considerably with our overstimulated culture today.

So advertising is everywhere. Every coffee shop window, lamppost, subway tunnel, baseball hat, side of a bus, food store bag, hundred-year-old maple tree, and name of a college football halftime report has become a potential place for marketing a product. Blank space is becoming an endangered species. We have supermarket eggs stamped with names of TV shows, receipts with advertisements for restaurants on the back, ads for watches in the trays at airport security screenings, and advertising space sold on motion sickness bags on planes.

Some companies have even toyed with the idea of using high power lasers to project advertisements onto the moon's surface.

When you see a NASCAR race, it's a blur of colors. "There goes the Cheerios car into the lead as Geico pulls into the pits and the Gatorade team gets their car back out on the track..." Everything is a blur. You hardly remember there's an eight hundred horsepower engine underneath the hood of the cars that's designed for one primary purpose, winning the race.

I wonder if we've done the same with Jesus. Rather than have him be the person to get others to learn about, have we made him the object to hang our marketing on? Have we "NASCAR-ified" Jesus and turned him into a blur of ads marketed towards the needs and desires of people with our Christian-based messages – how to have a good marriage, child rearing tips, healing, helping the homeless, community improvement, spiritual teaching, life direction coaching, counseling, kingdom financial planning, Christ-centered athletics, music with a purpose, political activism, eco-accountability – that we've forgotten what's under the hood and the primary purpose of why Jesus came?[44]

Have we made Jesus a CEO of a multi-faceted Christian bubble conglomerate? Have we made him into a spiritual Amazon.com? Anything you need, go to Jesus. This may sound too reckless or harsh to say. Nothing in God's creation or how it functions is insignificant to Jesus.

This is true, but we've tweaked him to the point that Jesus' top priority is everything and the obvious problem when everything is a priority is that nothing is a priority. All these good things need to serve the greater priority.

Arthur Glasser wrote "To make Jesus' model of Kingdom ministry the object of one's reflection and action means focusing on God's concern for God's world and the physical, social, and spiritual needs of others. Only by pursuing a Kingdom ministry can one keep 'churchly' activities in rightful subordination to the will of God."[45] When the early church did this, the impact as described by others was that these followers of Jesus had "turned the world upside down."[46]

Sixty-two times in his gospel, John uses the word *sent* or *send*. Fifty-four of those are in reference to either God sending Jesus out or Jesus sending his followers out. This word is used so often and so pointedly that it can't help but reveal the heart and mission of Jesus. It puts emphases on Jesus' purpose. The differences between a static church and one that "seeks first [God's] kingdom and his righteousness"[47] are described by Howard A. Snyder.

The church gets in trouble whenever it thinks it is in the church business rather than the Kingdom business. In the church business, people are concerned with the church activities, religious behavior and spiritual things. In the Kingdom business, people are concerned about Kingdom activities, all human behavior and everything God has made, visible and invisible. Kingdom people see human affairs as saturated with spiritual meaning and Kingdom significance. Kingdom people seek first the Kingdom of God and its justice; church people often put church work above concerns of justice, mercy, and truth. Church people think about how to get people into the church; Kingdom people think about how to get the church into the world. Church people worry that the world might change the church; Kingdom people work to see the church change the world...If the church has one great need, it is this: To be set free for the Kingdom of God, to be liberated from itself as it has become in order to be itself as God intends. The church must be freed to participate fully in the economy of God.[48]

~~~

I will never forget the simplest explanation of the Great Commission I ever heard. I was at a conference when Michael turned and said one word to me. "Throw." And then he just stared.

It was a little weird, but that is Michael's deadpan sense of humor. After a few seconds when he didn't say anything else, I raised my eyebrows and did a little head nod, the obvious body language saying "Man, I have *no* idea what you're talking about."

"Throw."

"All right. Throw…*what?*"

"Just throw." He kept saying this with a straight face. No explanation or clarifying. Just saying that single word. At first I thought it was some sort of joke I was being set up for. Then it started getting annoying. We're standing in the main hallway of this conference surrounded by display booths for mission trips. College students are wandering around talking to friends. There's worship music playing. And Michael just keeps saying "Throw."

"Throw *WHAT?*"

Then Michael looked at me with this 'I've got your attention now' look. "Verbs can't stand alone. Most of the talks we hear about the Great Commission focus on the main verb *make disciples*. But it can't be by itself and mean much. Like throw. Throw what? How? Where?"

This took on new clarity for me when I was coaching my daughter's seventh grade softball team. The girls already knew the answers to these 'throw' questions. When the ball was hit to the outfield, the parents, the players, the coaches all yell "Throw it!" and no other information needs to be given. Throw. What? The ball. How? Fast. Where? First base. When? Now! THROW! It's all a seamlessly understood action.

Contrast this with my youngest son's first year playing baseball. A bunch of five year olds are bent over digging in the dirt, baseball gloves are on top of their heads, and they're wondering what the snack after the game is going to be. The outfielders are tossing rocks at each other.

Then *WHACK* somebody actually hits the ball and it rolls into the outfield! Every parent starts yelling "Throw it!", but little Jimmy is standing there and has no idea what to do and starts running in place like he has to go to the bathroom. So the coach yells instructions. "Jimmy, get the ball! Pick it up! Now throw it to first base. No, don't run with it! Stop! Throw it. Throw it hard!" As the ball ends up going somewhere between second and third base, the coach yells "Great job, Jimmy! Hey, buddy, the next time the ball comes to you, I want you to…" and he tells him exactly what to do. He's teaching him the fundamentals of baseball. Get your glove ready. Know what to do when the ball comes to you. Know what base to throw it to. Be ready.

"Go and make disciples of all nations…" Make disciples. How? By going. Where? To the nations, which simply means *peoples*, not geography with boundary lines drawn. Which people? All of them. We often chop off that *all nations* part, but this go making disciples requires us to embrace the *all* – the people physically far away in another country, and the people nearby within our community that we overlook or are uncomfortable around – where disciples aren't being made yet.[49] Disciple-making was never meant to be a passive, misunderstood verb. Discipleship and being a follower of Jesus are symmetrical with mission.

Jesus didn't say "Go make disciples. I don't care how." That makes no sense at all, just like t*hrow* standing alone without any context means you can throw anywhere in any way and it should be ok. The ability to throw a ball hard and fast isn't the goal of baseball and means nothing by itself. This action only accomplishes the bigger goal when it's understood in the context of a baserunner racing to first base and the concept of an out is understood. The desire to win the game is the compelling drive that changes a casual toss to anywhere in the field into a bullet shot into the glove of an outstretched first baseman. When the umpire says, "Out!", the full meaning of "throw" makes sense. The final score is the goal and the throw to first base is the critical and fundamental action any ballplayer needs to be able to do from anywhere on the field in order to win the game. Games aren't won by throwing really fast but in the wrong direction.

~~~

Jesus' view of making disciples is very proactive, directed, intentional, initiative-taking, opportunity-seeking. Passivity doesn't accomplish a whole lot.

Our kids have tried lemonade sales in our driveway several times. Usually they make about $3, half of which comes from one neighbor and the other half is me buying back my own lemonade like a good dad. But they try. The problem is we live on a street with almost no traffic.

One Saturday, they had been sitting in the driveway for two hours and I was eyeing the money jar thinking I should go buy a few cups. Then the unplanned happened.

There are four ways to cross the river near our town. Three bridges and a ferry. We live less than a mile from the ferry. Guess what happens when all three bridges are closed on the same summer weekend? You get a *really* long line of cars outside our neighborhood waiting for the ferry. Guess what you get when you have people sitting in their cars for two or three hours on a hot Saturday afternoon waiting for that ferry?

"DAD! CAN WE GO SELL LEMONADE??!!" The kids scrambled for pitchers and lemonade mix, loaded up the red wagon with a cooler, made posters, and plastered their little brother with signs that said "The Big Lemon. 50 cents a glass."

Then they walked up and down a half mile stretch of road, hawking their ice cold drinks to ferry-waiting hostages. An hour later they came back with empty pitchers, no more lemonade mix, and $66. If you want to sell lemonade, you go to where people are thirsty, not at the end of your driveway where there's no traffic.

In our Matthew 9 verses, Jesus says there is a huge harvest ready. Jesus doesn't tell his followers to pray for the fields to ripen in the future. They aren't waiting to get ripe. These fields – people Jesus sees in every town and village he goes to – are men and women and children ready. They are looking to let go of their spiritual emptiness, ready to begin their search for some hope; they are asking for something to believe in, or wanting to replace whatever slowly deflating life preserver they are holding onto. "Peter, Andrew, Thaddeus, guys, look around us. Why do you think people are here? They're searching for something. Have you noticed that each and every village has been like that? Are you seeing what I'm seeing? It's consistently *everywhere*."

Crop readiness is not the issue. Manpower is. Jesus' appeal is not about the end results. Those are already a given. What is not assumed are workers going where crops are ready, which is such a bizarre thing to realize happens. If you drove down a road and saw crops of corn or tomatoes starting to rot, you'd think "What a waste." A smart landowner hires people and sends them to work in different parts of his field, not all into one location. Too many workers in one section and you have people overlapping work, running into each other, or standing around. At the same time, the other ready crops are expiring. It's counterproductive, the proverbial "too many cooks in the kitchen".

This is a problem for the church. We have moved from loading up a wagon full of coolers and lemonade pitchers and going to where thirsty people are and instead are waiting at the end of our driveways settling for $3 pocket change from Dad who already drinks too much lemonade. Or, put as a question, is most of what my church is doing working where work is already being done by others, or are we looking *at the same time* for ripe fields with not enough workers in them?

This may sound blunt, but it is a question we should be asking if we are talking about going where Jesus is going. I am not saying we shouldn't focus on making disciples of those within our churches. Remember the words Isaiah heard from God about the bigger picture as it relates to Jesus' mission. God said, "It is too small a thing for you to be my servant to restore the tribes of Jacob and bring back those of Israel I have kept. I will *also* make you a light for the Gentiles, that you may bring my salvation to the ends of the earth."[50] There is no either-or for God. "I need you to be making disciples of those who know me as well as those who do not yet, of those close by and those out of earshot, of those where things are happening and where they aren't yet. I need workers continuing here to harvest and I need workers to go to those fields that are waiting to be harvested before they expire."

There's a great line at the beginning of the movie *Seabiscuit*. In the early 1900's, the introduction of the automobile brought the birth of the manufacturing assembly line. Cars were quickly produced to match the increasing demand of the public. The first Model T's took thirteen hours to assemble. Within five years, Henry Ford had perfected the assembly line and was turning out a vehicle every ninety minutes.

Other industries soon began assembly line production. For generations, fathers and mothers had taught sons and daughters the intricacies of making something and taking pride in it. Now "seamstresses became button sewers. Furniture makers became knob turners." A man who had once hand stitched leather seats or had worked with a lathe to make carriage wheels was now worker #17, responsible for putting hubcaps on wheels as they passed in front of him. The narrator concludes with a simple statement that leaves you sad and unsettled: "It was the beginning and the end of imagination, all at the same time."[51]

Has that become true of God's church? Have we become simply good hubcappers instead of carriage makers? Have we become good at building our body, but not building the church? How would it disrupt our norm if we asked ourselves, "Is what we are doing locally connecting us with those who are not connected?" Where are 90% of churches in my city already doing ministry? What demographic is being left out because it might be harder to connect with them?[52]

Do people in our church or ministry feel they can try something we haven't done before; or, maybe more importantly, have we asked what they are passionate about doing to connect with others outside the church? Is our church or ministry a place where we intentionally and visibly support "new" things to go to the ready fields? Have we created space for these things? Do people feel prepared to talk with those who don't know God yet in the classrooms, offices, construction sites, dorms, stores, and playgrounds God puts them in five or six days out of the week? In trying to be more culturally relevant on Sundays have we become less intentional the rest of the week?

What we celebrate reflects who we are, but what we celebrate also shapes what we become. It's cyclical and self-feeding. Celebration leads to encouragement and wonder, which leads to people feeling invited to try new things, and then we circle back to celebrating what God has done and is doing. Do we celebrate enough, and do we celebrate enough of the right things? What do we learn when we see that each of the three stories of lost things being found that Jesus told in Luke 15 (a sheep, a coin, a son) all end with Jesus saying something about the excessive celebration in heaven when a lost person is found? Does that celebration reflect something about priorities of the kingdom? Are we settling for too small? Do we really believe that Sunday morning church attendance or our weekly campus meeting accurately reflects the spiritual hunger in our town, and if not are we willing to do things differently?

Am I willing to evaluate how much of my church's local and global engagement is connecting and serving people that others can't or won't? Where is the field showing it's ripe but doesn't have enough workers, and how can my church, my campus ministry, my small group, my family join believers who are there? What could three musical teenagers do if they were given ten guitars and encouraged to give free lessons to ten kids who come from homes where they are financially struggling enough that they might never get the chance to play an instrument? What if these three teens got to build trust with the families, did a show at the end of a few months for their parents, gave the guitars away, and built relationships showing and sharing Christ with them? What if the same happened when retired men who love tinkering on cars started offering free oil changes, rotating tires, and basic maintenance in a section of town, mentoring young people at the same time in basic auto repair so the kids can learn a simple skill, and built intentional relationships? What if Christian artists initiated a "theme a month" for the arts community in town and at the end of each month at a coffee shop each artist was given a few minutes to explain how that painting, photo, or drawing captured that theme's idea for them, building relationships that invite us to hear their story more fully?

Are we ready to ask "How does this particular one week mission trip really help in making disciples within my church?" If it's not, are we willing to change who we are doing trips with or what we do on those trips? Rather than using mission trips as stand-alone events for the church, how do they also fit into intentional steps towards reaching a disconnected niche within our own community? Have we told our pastors "We want you to go overseas for ten days every year" so they bring a fresh perspective to their teaching that stretches us? Or send our children's ministry volunteers so they can begin sharing a global heart with children in our church? Has our church studied global and local mission trends and are we moving to carry them forward or entrenching in our historic approaches because they are comfortable?[53]

The early church didn't settle for small things. They didn't hubcap. They didn't say in dull monotone "All we do is make disciples." They could have been comfortable, gathering safe people into safe bubbles and doing very good, safe, acceptable, non-disruptive things. But they themselves knew there was more. They remembered that they had been outsiders to the spiritual "safe bubble" before. That's what I believe compelled them to closely echo through their actions Paul's words in Romans 15. "It has always been my *ambition* to preach the gospel where Christ was not known, so that I would not be building on someone else's foundation."[54] An ambition – a goal, a dream, a desire – comes from a restless heart that sees opportunity, not from sitting along an assembly line mundanely putting in time.

Have we lost something? Some perspective that has drifted a little way from shore and we didn't notice? Are we hubcapping, or are we building something beautiful? Are we at a place where we can hear Jesus saying, "Talitha koum" to people? When's the last time we walked into a field that was ripe, ready, and saw hardly anybody else already working there?

If, like the four friends of the paralyzed man, you could do *whatever it takes* to get a person or a group of people into the house to see Jesus, what would you do?

Impressions have consequences

To bring all this to a conclusion, we return to Tolkien's world of the *Lord of the Rings…*

And so it was happening again in The Shire. Frodo's Uncle Bilbo Baggins had told the story many times to the young hobbit. Bilbo had been outside this very house and minding his own business when into his safe, neat, predictable world came the wizard Gandalf. The story that followed that uncomplicated beginning was frightening and amazing and breathtaking to the young hobbit who could only imagine what lay beyond the Shire border past Brandywine River. His uncle – a fine upstanding stay-at-home simple Baggins – ended up doing unthinkable things, things that made no sense to well-earthed hobbits.

Frodo had often dreamed of travel. He wanted adventures like Uncle Bilbo's! They seemed so real but fantastical at the same time. Over the years, respectable hobbits who had heard all these tales too many times had begun calling the elder Bilbo silly and batty, a bit crazed. And now his nephew was showing hints of this madness too, poor lad.

Frodo often daydreamed of what it would be like to wander through meadows spreading wide open before him, or into endless forests, or walk through dark unknown caves, or to see the stars from the very tops of mountains, or to listen to the music of elves.

But now here it was. This same Gandalf sitting by his fire in Bag End puffing his pipe. Waiting for Frodo's answer.

Suddenly adventure seemed too big for a small hobbit. He hadn't imagined that for Bilbo's story to be his own it would mean taking his life into his hands, going from the known to the unknown, safety to danger.

The Ring must be destroyed. Its maker, the Dark Lord Sauron, was seeking it out at all costs. It must be taken into distant Mordor and tossed into the Cracks of Doom before he could find it and use it for his own purposes, the end of Middle Earth.

And somehow this very Ring had ended up in the Shire. In the waistcoat of Frodo, who was at this moment fingering it in his pocket. Gandalf sat silently, puffing smoke rings, waiting.

"Well!" said Gandalf, looking up at last. "Have you decided what to do?"[55]

~ ~ ~

We all know there is a point where we need to decide to do something. It is each person's invitation and dilemma. It is comfortable to study about Jesus, to talk about what Jesus must have seen, felt, prayed, and done, and the why's that compelled him. But the difference-making question – the disturbing one – is "Am I more like him?" Isn't that the goal of being a follower of somebody? Has who that person is become impressed upon me?

If you remember from the beginning of this book, I shared how the verses in Matthew 9 began a whittling process on me as I read them one cold night in college. After two hours, I finally stood up from my perch overlooking campus, wiped the snow off, and began walking nowhere specifically, asking myself "Have I become more like Jesus – seeing as he saw, feeling as he felt?"

But I really needed to wrestle with that, not letting it just get the quick "of course" response, because if I was going to go there, there was a risk. Would I be willing to pray as Jesus prayed?

But there was a risk in that question too, because Jesus prayed for laborers, and the question I knew that would come was, "Tim, what if I want you to be an answer to your own prayers? Are you willing to go do what Jesus did, wherever and whatever that might be?" This was no longer a conversation God and I were having about what career path to take. It was deeper. It was personal.

And, if I was willing to ask those questions, there would be yet more risk, because by doing as Jesus did, this whole thing would circle back around, giving me new opportunities and situations to see people even more clearly, feeling deeper compassion and unsettledness, and so on, continuing this never-ending cycle required to become more like Jesus. Or I could stop it right now and by default stay where I felt safe.

Andrew Jackson, who was a US Army General in the early 1800's and later became seventh President of the United States, was asked what word of advice drawn from his experience in serving the country would he give to a group of Congressmen starting their careers. He wrote back, "Always take all the time to reflect that circumstances permit, but when the time for action has come, stop thinking." What a great word of advice to pass on to the church and each Christ-follower.

John Eldridge asks in *Wild At Heart,*

> If you had permission to do what you really want to do, what would you do? Don't ask how, that will cut your desire off at the knees. How is never the right question; how is a faithless question. It means "unless I can see my way clearly I won't believe it, won't venture forth."...How is God's department. He is asking you what. What is written in your heart?[56]

What do you believe God is inviting you to join him in?

This sort of question is dangerous. It's like seeing a loose corner of a canvas painting that's been hanging on your wall for years and peeling it back just enough to see the very edge of something written underneath. What is it? If you knew peeling more of the original painting would reveal something new underneath, but it would also mean the original painting wouldn't be restored to its previous condition, would you? Or would you press the corner down and hang the picture back on the wall and be content to wonder what is underneath it? Could you sit in that room and not be curious?

It's an annoying inconvenience that we cannot stay where we are and go with God at the same time.[57] There is nothing that can facilitate such a simultaneous experience. Rather, we need to allow ourselves to be interrupted by God. Henry Blackaby draws attention to how this has always been the nature of God's invitation.

Noah could not continue life as usual and build an ark at the same time. Abram could not stay in Ur or Haran and father a nation in Canaan. Moses could not stay on the back side of the desert herding sheep and stand before Pharaoh at the same time. David had to leave his sheep to become king…Jonah had to leave his home and overcome a major prejudice in order to preach to Nineveh. Peter, Andrew, James, and John had to leave their fishing business in order to follow Jesus. Matthew had to leave his tax collector's booth to follow Jesus. Saul (later Paul) had to completely change directions in his life in order to be used by God to preach the gospel to the Gentiles.

Any involvement wherever and to whomever God invites us is the place where theology and practice meet. Practice without theology is hollow; theology without practice will become extinct. We haven't been called to either hollowness or extinction. As John, one of Jesus' closest followers during his ministry years, wrote,

> "If anyone obeys his word,
> God's love is truly made complete in him.
> This is how we know we are in him:
> Whoever claims to live in him must walk as Jesus did."

I John 2:5-6 (NIV)

And Jesus went.

Where stuff came from

1 I have heard this used many times but wanted to make sure it wasn't an urban legend quote. Thanks to Coca-Cola for sending me an original of The Coca-Cola 1993 Annual Report to verify. This quote appears on page 8.

2 John 7:37, NASB.

3 Malcolm Gladwell, *The Tipping Point: How Little Things Can Make A Big Difference* (New York: Brown and Co., 2000), 92.

4 C.S. Lewis, *Mere Christianity* (New York: Touchstone – Simon & Schuster, 1996), 121.

5 In the West, we tend to focus on the individual and miss this bigger interrelated state of brokenness. James Choung uses a narrative writing style in *True Story: A Christianity Worth Believing In* (Downers Grove, IL: InterVarsity Press, 2008) to give readers an excellent diagram drawn on a napkin so that they can share this with people not yet following Jesus.

6 Acts 27:13-20.

7 Luke 17:1-2, NIV, emphasis my own.

8 2 Peter 3:9, 1 Timothy 2:3-6.

9 The story of Jesus, Jairus, and his daughter can be found in Matthew 9:18-26, Mark 5:21-43 and Luke 8:40-56.

10 David E. Garland, *The NIV Application Commentary: Mark* (Grand Rapids, MI: Zondervan, 1996), 222.

11 N. T. Wright, *Mark for Everyone.* 2nd ed. (Louisville, KY: Westminster John Knox Press, 2004), 63.

12 I am aware that in using the story of Jairus, some people will say I am advocating simple positive thinking to see spiritual

results. I am not. There are no assumptions Jairus could make. Hope for, yes. But Jesus didn't tell Jairus "Your daughter will get better," or "...will come back to life", or anything about his daughter for that matter. He had no promises that all would end well. The main point of this biblical story is similar to others in the gospels, just dressed differently. A paralytic lowered through the roof comes for healing but has his bigger spiritual issues addressed as well (Mark 2:1-12, Luke 5:17-26). A woman caught in adultery needs rescuing, but receives affirmation of value (John 8:1-11). A bleeding woman is healed, but is called "daughter", restored after twelve years of being an outcast in the social and religious communities (in the middle of the story of Jairus in Matthew 9, Mark 5, and Luke 8). All of these have a common big picture story of faith journey or personal relationship with God. But it would be wrong to avoid the other things we can see within the sub-stories. In Jairus' story, I can't avoid seeing the wrestling he goes through between hope and resignation as he hears the news, walks the road back to his home, enters the room with his dead daughter on a mat, and then hears Jesus say, "Talitha koum." I do believe a lesson to be taken away is that what seems so ridiculously difficult, so impregnably sealed, is not to God. The miraculous overcoming of impossible obstacles is normative for God.

[13] Mark 10:45, NLT.

[14] John 3:16, NLT.

[15] John 17:3, MSG.

[16] John 10:14-16, NLT.

[17] Matthew 4:19, NLT.

[18] John 17:18, NLT.

[19] Acts 1:8, NLT. Jesus clearly defines the scope of God's

mission – Jerusalem (the immediate home area), Judea (the larger surrounding area), Samaria (the hated semi-related, semi-foreigners next door), and to the ends of the earth.

20 Matthew 28:18-19, NLT.

21 I like the wording used in used Matthew 24:14, MSG, "The Message of the kingdom will be preached all over the world, *a witness staked out in every country*," (emphasis my own) which I think is a good image for the "Will everybody respond?" question. The gospel message will be present among people but may not be pervasive as people choose not to embrace it.

22Arthur F Glasser, *Announcing the Kingdom: The Story of God's Mission in the Bible.* 2007 ed. (Grand Rapids, MI: Baker Academic, 2003), 193.

23 Luke 14:15-24.

24 Matthew 10:16, NIV.

25 Nik Ripken and Gregg Lewis, *The Insanity of God: A True Story of Faith Resurrected* (Nashville, TN: B&H Group, 2013), 140.

26 Matthew 25:14-30.

27 Henry T. Blackaby and Claude V. King, *Experiencing God* (Nashville, TN: Holman, 1994), 150.

28 J.R.R. Tolkien, *The Fellowship of the Ring* (New York: Del Rey, 2012), 67.

29 Blake Snyder, *Save the Cat!: The Last Book on Screenwriting That You'll Ever Need* (Studio City, CA: Michael Wiese Productions, 2005), 31.

30 Acts 3:1-4:13.

31 John 15:5, translation by N. T. Wright, *John for Everyone, Part 2 Chapters 11-21.* 2nd ed. (Louisville, KY: Westminster John Knox Press, 2004), 68.

32 Three accounts of Jesus and the paralyzed man are found in Matthew 9:2-8, Mark 2:1-12, Luke 5:17-26.

33 Peter was one of Jesus' most passionate followers and also a

fisherman from Capernaum, Matthew 8. Some scholars believe that the house where Jesus met the paralyzed man may have been Peter's.

34 Timothy J. Keller, *King's Cross: The Story of the World in the Life of Jesus* (New York: Dutton Redeemer, 2011), 28.

35 Mark 2:9, NIV.

36 Mark 2:10, MSG.

37 There are three accounts of Jesus raising people from the dead (besides being raised himself) – Jairus' daughter (Matthew 9, Mark 5, Luke 8), his friend Lazarus (John 11), and a widow's son (Luke 7).

38 Christopher J. H. Wright, *The Mission of God: Unlocking the Bible's Grand Narrative* (Downers Grove, IL: IVP Academic, 2006), 22.

39 John 15:5, MSG.

40 Isaiah 49:6, NIV, emphasis my own.

41 Isaiah 49:6, MSG.

42 Matthew 4:19 and Mark 1:17, NIV. Jesus also says this to the rich young man in Matthew 19:21, Mark 10:21, and Luke 18:22 but the man can't get to the point of doing it.

43 David Platt, *Follow Me: A Call to Die. A Call to Live* (Carol Stream, IL: Tyndale House, 2013), 16.

44 Let me make sure I'm heard correctly. The Jesus that I read about fed people, healed sick ones, and showed overflowing care for those who were suffering. At the same time, he was teaching people and telling his followers to go into the world and make disciples. You can't separate the two. Jesus was strong in words and deeds, "serving" and "saving". Unfortunately, the pendulum swings in our culture. In the late 20th century, the church largely left the social care of the poor, homeless, and hurting to others and focused on what was

called "evangelistic work" or the "real ministry" of gospel proclamation. As the 21st century started, more of the church took ownership of its role in community improvement, meeting critical life needs of people, and seeking social justice. While medical care, food programs, and literacy programs will not restore the spiritual relationship of a person with God, they should not be ignored by the church. Clean water, no AIDS, and a school for every child are things for which we should strive. The church should be the one that people – no matter their belief, lifestyle, worldview, -ism, or -ology – looks at and says "These people show more love to us than anybody else, even if they don't get anything out of it for themselves."

However, care needs to be taken to make sure the pendulum finds the middle. In the last half-century of increased attention to "social gospel" work, children are being fed, young girls are being rescued from the sex trade, and micro-businesses are providing for families in slums, but all the deeper things causing these situations in the first place still remain strong and foreboding realities. If these are not addressed, has anything really changed? These difficult tasks may bring about community transformation and improve lives, but they cannot accomplish God's mission of intentionally seeking to restore people and make things right without a discipleship and evangelistic focus brought alongside them. The Great Commandment (Love the Lord with all your heart, soul, mind, and strength, and love you neighbor as yourself...) and the Great Commission (Go make disciples...) don't go hand-in-hand as two separate things joined together for convenience. They are synonymous.

How we as the church address these critical issues that remain unchecked in our world is not the focus of this book, but it is a direct action and response we should have if we are becoming more like Jesus. Some challenging books to read on this are David Platt's *Radical* and *Radical Together* as well as Timothy Keller's *Generous Justice: How God's Grace Makes Us Just.* There are also the very practical ones by Steve Corbett and Brian Fikkert's *When Helping Hurts: How To Alleviate Poverty Without Hurting The Poor...And Yourself* and Robert Lupton's *Toxic Charity: How Churches and Charities Hurt Those They Help (And How To Reverse It).*

[45] Glasser 200.

[46] Acts 17:6, ESV.

[47] Matthew 6:33, NIV.

[48] Quoted in Glasser, 200.

[49] We have Jerusalems, Judias, Samarias, and the ends of the earth represented within our communities, our campuses and schools, our work places, our civic groups, the coffee shop we spend time at, and our kids' teams.

[50] Isaiah 49:6, NIV, emphasis my own.

[51] *Seabiscuit*, Dir. Gary Ross, Perf. Tobey Maguire and Jeff Bridges, Universal Studios, 2003.

[52] David Platt took his church, The Church at Brook Hills in Birmingham, AL, here. Even though they are in the heart of the "American Bible Belt" and in a church-filled, ministries-everywhere city, Brook Hills and individuals in it sought places in Birmingham and beyond that weren't being touched by the church. The theological underpinnings and experiences that stretched an already established "successful" church are written in his books *Radical* and *Radical Together.*

[53] A good book to read that prompts these sorts of global mission questions is Paul Borthwick's *Western Christians in Global Missions: What's the Role of the North American Church?* (Downers Grove, IL: InterVarsity Press, 2012).

There are several books and articles that share research about global trends in missions, especially highlighting the growth of both indigenous laborers working in and sent laborers going from the Global South (historically lesser developed countries in the southern portion of the globe including Africa, India, parts of Asia, and South/Central America). A quick online read is Melissa Steffan, "The Surprising Countries Most Missionaries Are Sent From And Go To," *Christianity Today*, June 26, 2013, www.christianitytoday.com/gleanings/ 2013/july/missionaries-countries-sent-received-csgc-gordon-conwell.html (accessed June 26, 2015).

Another book that I would highly recommend is Philip Jenkins, *The Next Christendom: The Coming Global Christianity* (New York: Oxford University Press, 2007). Other books on the changing look of world missions that include chapters on the Global South growth can be found on Amazon.com, but Jenkins devotes a whole book with ample statistics, quotes, and research. While it is a little older now, a reader wanting to gain a deep immersion into this can't go wrong here.

I also recommend the fifteen week Perspectives on the World Christian Movement course. It is hosted by approximately 200 churches in the US each year. For information or to locate a course, visit www.perspectives.org.

54 Romans 15:20, NIV, emphasis my own.

55 The description here is adapted from Kurt Bruner and Jim Ware, *Finding God in The Lord of the Rings* (Wheaton, IL: Tyndale House, 2001), 11.

56 John Eldridge, *Wild At Heart: Discovering the Secret of a Man's Soul* (Nashville: Thomas Nelson Publishers, 2001), 206.

57 A variation of Blackaby, 147.

Acknowledgements

Nothing gets done well when attempted in a vacuum.

I am particularly indebted to the team of prayer and financial supporters who have been with us for several years in our ministry. Many of you have prodded me to write. Thank you for doing so.

If you are blessed with friends who over the long haul encourage you to try new things, hold onto them. Clif Brigham, Alan Clark, Andy Cronan, Rick James and Bruce Utne have been long-time catalysts for moving ramblings into ideas into substance, this book being but one example.

Without nudging by friends and family, the editing of Katie Carpenter, and last minute graphic help from Elizabeth Holcomb this would have continued sitting in a box in my garage propping up a leaning water heater.

Of course, my family – particularly my bride, Kathy – provided boosts when I was frustrated, cheers when I needed them, and (sometimes) quiet to write. Thank you.

On my desk is a small piece of paper that says, "Write as an act of worship, not a project." That is how I hope this has been received by God.

About the author

Tim grew up along the East Coast of the US, pretended that he could play basketball as a teenager before switching to hurdles, and developed a serious obsession for sweet tea. In college he studied civil engineering and decided to spend just two years in full-time ministry after graduation. Twenty-eight years later, Tim has no idea how to build a bridge anymore. Instead, he spent many years with Cru launching movements on college campuses in the U.S. Eventually, he got his MA in Intercultural Studies and began partnering with native church planters in countries where it is difficult to be a Christ follower. He's working on his PhD and helping start a local ministry center using creative communication and coffee to connect with the community. He and his wife, Kathy, have four children in college and high school and live in Virginia. He is still obsessed with sweet tea.

Tim can be contacted at BarefootNomadLLC@gmail.com.

29761612R00071

Made in the USA
Lexington, KY
03 February 2019